TRANSRACIAL ADOPTION
CHILDREN
AND
PARENTS SPEAK

TRANSRACIAL ADOPTION

CHILDREN AND PARENTS SPEAK

by Constance Pohl and Kathy Harris

FRANKLIN WATTS
NEW YORK • CHICAGO • LONDON • TORONTO • SYDNEY

Cover photograph copyright © Randy Matusow

Photographs on pp. 4, 6 top, 7 top, 8, 9 top are courtesy of the families;
pp. 11, 12, 13, 14 are courtesy of Children's Aid and Adoption Society/Sal
Benedetto; All other photographs copyright © Randy Matusow.

Library of Congress Cataloging-in-Publication Data:

Pohl, Constance.
Transracial adoption : children and parents speak / by Constance
Pohl and Kathy Harris.
p.   cm.
Includes bibliographical references and index.
Summary: Explores the issues related to interracial and
international adoptions, using interviews with black, biracial,
Asian, and Hispanic young people who were adopted into white or
biracial families.
ISBN 0-531-11134-2
1. Interracial adoption—United States—Juvenile literature.
2. Intercountry adoption—United States—Juvenile literature.
[1. Interracial adoption. 2. Intercountry adoption. 3. Adoption.]
I. Harris, Kathy   II. Title.
HV875.64.P65   1992
362.7'34—dc20   92-10991 CIP AC

CONTENTS

ACKNOWLEDGMENTS

This book would not have been possible without the immense generosity of the families interviewed here. They shared their experiences and gave of their time with unfailing courtesy. We are indebted to them all. We have chosen to change their names as we present their stories and comments.

We also wish to thank Jeanne Vestal for the opportunity to publish this book, and Lorna Greenberg for her indispensable editing skill, and Randy Matusow and Caroline Anderson for the sensitive photography.

C.P.
K.H.

TRANSRACIAL ADOPTION
CHILDREN
AND
PARENTS SPEAK

INTRODUCTION

Transracial adoption is the adoption of a child of one race by parents of another race. In the 1960s, significant numbers of white parents began to adopt African American children. The controversy that arose over this practice should not surprise us, in light of the history of the United States. As recently as 1967 miscegenation—a black person marrying a white person—was a crime in sixteen southern states. Until 1954 the segregation of black children and white children in separate schools was permitted under federal law. Even today racist incidents occur on many American college campuses, and many communities are still divided into black and white neighborhoods.

Given this legacy, black activists and social workers have questioned whether white parents can successfully raise an African American child. Some African American social workers have called transracial adoption harmful to the African American community.

The critics pointed out that children must develop positive racial identities in order to feel good about themselves, and this is difficult for black children in white families. Adopted children need suitable African American role models, education about African American culture and history, and skills to cope with racism. In 1972 the Association of Black Social Workers denounced the practice of crossracial adoptions.

As a result of these objections, adoption agencies placed a virtual ban on the adoption of black children by white parents. State social service agencies instituted regulations, many of which are still in effect, requiring that the race of the adoptive parents be matched to the child's. For example, a New York State regulation says that a child must be placed with adoptive parents of the same religion, race, and ethnic background.

All advocates for children know that caring, competent parents are essential for a child. What then is to be done if no black family is available to adopt a black child, and there is a white family who wants to adopt this child? Should the child be placed with the white family, or should the child be kept waiting for years for a black adoptive parent who may never arrive? This is another aspect of the controversy surrounding transracial adoption.

What can we learn about transracial adoption? The children adopted in the United States before the mid-1970s, as well as children adopted from foreign countries, have grown up in transracial families and learned firsthand about its difficulties and its merits.

In the chapters that follow, young adults and their parents, and brothers and sisters in transracial adoptive families, share with us their experiences: the difficulties, mistakes, and pain; and the successes, rewards, and joys. Through their words, we explore some aspects of this difficult yet heartening relationship.

THE FAMILIES

Gary Lewis, African American, adopted 1972
Brian Lewis, African American, adopted 1974

Monique Lewis, biracial, adopted 1981
Leslie Lewis, white, adoptive mother
Frank Lewis, African American, adoptive father

Sean Murphy, African American–Irish American, adopted
    1972
Dierdre Murphy, biological daughter, born 1977
Jenny Murphy, biological daughter, born 1969
Karen and Joseph Murphy, white, adoptive parents

Jody Simns, biracial, adopted 1973
Rachel Simns, white, adoptive mother

Cal, Tanzanian 1973, adopted 1986
Laura and James, white, adoptive parents

Lola Girard, Senegalese, adopted 1974
Marie-Claire Girard, French Canadian, adoptive mother

Sheila Marcel, Bangladeshi, adopted 1975
French Canadian adoptive parents

Mark Lorenzo, biracial, adopted 1976
Steven Lorenzo, African American, adopted 1977
Two Hispanic adopted daughters
Julie and Robert Lorenzo, white, adoptive parents

Mark Soule, African American, adopted before 1972
four white adopted children and two black adopted children
Peggy Soule, white, adoptive mother

Ben Adams, Korean, adopted 1975
Two biological daughters
Ann and Fred Adams, white, adoptive parents

Damien Cohen, Brazilian, adopted 1986
Peter Cohen, Brazilian, adopted 1988
Carey Cohen, white, adoptive father

Rafael James, Brazilian, adopted 1984
Cecilia James, biological daughter, born 1976
Alice James, white, adoptive mother

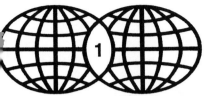

GARY LEWIS: ADOPTION AT THE AGE OF FIVE

Unlike most of us, Gary Lewis has a very special memory: he can remember seeing his mother for the very first time, when he was five years old.

"The first time I met my mother we went to a playground," Gary recalls. "The next time, she took me out to the zoo. I remember running around. And then I remember coming home and seeing my own room. It was pretty big and had all kinds of toys in it, so it was pretty nice.

"I was confused a lot. I wondered what was going on. I remember being brought down to the Center—the adoption agency—and the people were explaining all kinds of things I didn't understand. About my feelings—I know I was glad and also a little sad. I left this little girl I was with all the time at the other house. I think she was my sister."

Naturally, Gary's mother also remembers this first meeting. "It was September, and we spent the afternoon in Central Park in New York City," she recalls. "I had the feeling that everything was just right, that he was the right kid. I thought to myself that if I'd had a biological child, I couldn't have gotten it this right. I was charmed by Gary; he looked so gorgeous to me. I was afraid it was too good to be real.

"There is a memory I have from the first day in the park. We were riding on the carousel, and Gary started to slide off his horse. I reached over and stopped him from falling. At that moment I had a flash: I thought, From now on, I will always be able to take care of you. I believed he needed me as much as I needed him.

"Two days later we had a second visit at the aquarium. Then he came to my home for an afternoon and returned to spend the weekend with me. On Sunday when the social worker picked him up to take him back to his foster home, she asked him if he wanted to stay at my house. He answered yes, so the worker said, 'Then we'll arrange that.' Two days later Gary came to stay for good—twelve days after our first meeting!''

In 1992 Gary Lewis is twenty-five, a teacher and counselor at a private residential school for young men who have been in trouble with the law. Each of these adolescents has committed a crime, been placed on probation by the courts, and then violated the probation or refused to return to school. Some of the boys, who come from all across the nation, have committed a second crime. They have had hard young lives, and Gary is able to help them and work with them because the odds were against him in his life, too.

In his first five years Gary lived with three different foster families before finally being adopted by his white mother. Each of the three moves from foster homes felt like a rejection and left him emotionally scarred. These feelings of early abandonment created more difficulty in the adoption than did the racial difference. However, Gary's story is an example of how an understanding adoptive parent can help a child survive and grow.

Leslie was unmarried when she adopted Gary. A single white woman adopting a five-year-old African American child was unusual in 1972. How did Leslie decide she wanted to do this?

"I was thirty years old in 1972, and marriage wasn't on the horizon, but I knew I wanted to be a parent. I was working at a large New York City hospital as a social worker. The week after I turned thirty I applied to a prominent adoption agency. I was very clear in my description of the child I wanted to adopt because I had thought about it for a long time. I could take a child who was not white, from toddler to kindergarten age. I had decided that an infant would be too hard for me to care for while working. During the home study interviews, the adoption agency social worker asked me how I'd decided I wanted to adopt and why I'd asked for a nonwhite child. I wanted to adopt a child who would not otherwise have a family, and I believed white children would be adopted regardless of their age or problems. I applied for a girl because I didn't think I'd be considered for a boy. I believed I could handle a child considered emotionally disturbed, but not a child who was physically handicapped. Through my work at the hospital, I knew how much care and medical attention a physically handicapped child would need. From my experience with children who have emotional problems, I felt I could parent such a child."

The people at the adoption agency liked Leslie and thought she would be a good parent, but they could not consider her for a nonwhite child because they did not place children across racial lines. They placed black children only with black parents. However, the agency wanted to help Leslie and suggested another agency which did still allow white families to adopt black children. In 1972 Leslie applied to the other adoption agency. The agency checked her references and carefully went over her application. A short time later she was contacted for an initial interview.

"The social worker asked, 'Could you consider a boy?' Boys were harder to place than girls, so that was their concern—finding a boy an adoptive home. For this reason the agency would consider allowing adoption across racial lines. After a discussion with a counselor, I told the social worker that I would take a boy.''

The initial interview is followed by a home study, a crucial part of the adoption process. A social worker visits the family home to see if it is a good place for a child to live. Among other things, the worker wanted to know if Leslie Lewis lived in a community that was suitable for a black child.

At the completion of the home study, the social worker described Gary to Leslie. That was in June. Three months later, in September, Gary came to Leslie's home to stay.

GARY'S FOSTER HOMES

Gary vaguely remembers the foster home where he lived before he was adopted. But like most memories from the age of four or five, the pictures are hazy, the facts are unclear, and everything appears larger than it would to adults.

"I can't remember faces too well,'' he says. "There were two boys who were brothers, and a girl who I think was my sister, and a woman. I slept in the last room up in the attic, and the woman slept in the other part of the attic. It was a huge house, and it had a big basement and a big kitchen.

"I don't remember the man clearly but a man lived there. He must have been my foster mother's husband. I think he worked at the airport. I remember taking late night drives to get ice cream. I guess it was Sunday nights.

"There must have been a Catholic school down the street, because lots of kids walked by the house in uniforms. The little girl and I would look out the window in the morning and see them going by.

"I spoke a lot of Spanish, because the foster family were Spanish-speaking people, so I had to learn English after I was adopted. My mother taught me English words. I guess I learned it fast. It wasn't hard for me.

"I wasn't attached to that foster home. I didn't feel they were my family. I don't remember feeling sad about leaving the adults, but I was sad because I thought I was leaving my sister. I was in one place, and then I was someplace else. I think I wondered why I didn't go back to the first house.

"After the adoption I wondered if I was going someplace new or going back to the house where I lived before. I wondered why I didn't go back to the first house. I kept asking my mother, 'Am I going back?' "

These moves early in life led to emotional troubles for young Gary. Emotionally troubled children are designated "hard to place" by adoption agencies because many would-be parents believe they cannot handle children with emotional problems.

Leslie anticipated difficulties. "I knew where Gary's emotional problems came from and how hurt he was by the moves he had been forced to make. One of his foster families truly cared for him but did not know how to cope with his problems.

"He couldn't tolerate frustration. When he had temper tantrums, I would hold him. At first he wet the bed every night, so we would just change the sheets every day.

"He liked to be carried all the time, even though he was big for his age. That was all right, because I knew he just wanted to be babied. I was attracted to his brightness and energy and his efforts to meet his own needs, so I didn't mind the other difficulties. I knew that eventually he would get better."

Leslie remembers that Gary loved to make cookies and that he enjoyed the stories she read to him. She bought clay for him, and he would spend hours molding it and then proudly show her what he had made.

"He was my kind of kid—very bright, sociable, active.

To me he was very appealing; he enjoyed the activities I offered, and he was very responsive to them.

" And I was right for him. He needed lots of attention, and with me he was the center of attention, so he had someone all to himself. Looking back, I would say that the social worker was excellent and did a good job of matching me and Gary.

"The early separations and the feelings of rejection that came with them were too much for Gary," she says. "Some children are more emotionally resilient, but Gary was vulnerable to those forced moves. To this day, fear of loss upsets him. Gary's greatest need was for a parent who could understand him and help him deal with his problems."

THE EFFECTS OF ABANDONMENT

Children who have been abandoned and neglected as infants and toddlers are scarred by the experience, and this must be recognized by anyone who adopts a child older than an infant. Almost all children adopted when older will have suffered some form of rejection.

Recent studies of how infants grow and learn have provided new insights into the way the human personality is shaped. In the first year of life children learn half of everything they will ever know. In those crucial first twelve months the infant is completely dependent on a primary caregiver—usually the mother. If a baby's needs for food and fluids, warmth, comfort, and nurture are consistently met, the baby will grow to trust the person providing the care. This trust allows the child to become attached to and to love the parent. The reverse, however, is also true. If the primary caregiver fails to meet the infant's needs, distrust grows in the child. Without the building blocks of trust, a child may not develop the ability to trust others and to love.

Each time a young child is taken away from a caregiver, the child's feelings are further injured, and the child's inability to trust is aggravated. Furthermore, this damage occurs at a time when the child should be developing the ability to think and learn. The motivation for learning comes from an urge to please a trusted person, but if a child does not trust and care for anyone, there is no one the child desires to please. Without this incentive to learn, the neglected child falls behind in language and learning skills. If, in addition, sexual or physical abuse occurs, the child is further distanced from those he or she may want to love.

The consequences of early abandonment and neglect can include such emotional problems, irrational fears, and learning disabilities. In extreme instances, the result can be an "unattached" child. In a less extreme case the child may learn to trust and yet be fearful of loss and wary of human relationships, or the child may have low self-esteem and feel unworthy of love.

BEING ADOPTED

Although Gary suffered from emotional problems, he was fortunate to have an adoptive parent who was patient and who understood his difficulties. "When I was little, I didn't know what adoption meant," Gary recalls. "I didn't know that someone else had had me and then left me. When I was a little older, I could understand. I was kind of curious about who my parents were. I asked questions because I wondered why they'd left me.

"I remember things like being at the doctor's. I was very tall for my age. The doctor told me I was going to be tall when I grew up. Then the doctor would say, 'Your father must have been tall.' And I would think to myself, How does he know my father? Does the doctor know who my father is?

"At first I thought that I was the only one in the world who had been adopted. Then I discovered it happened to other people, too. My Mom and I belonged to a group of single parents who had adopted children. I think it was good that my mother was in a group with other people who were like us. We often had picnics in the park. All the kids would run around and explore. I knew that park like the back of my hand. You learned you were like other kids in that group. Later Brian—my adopted brother—came along, and I could talk to him about being adopted.''

When a mother is white and her son is black, friends, schoolmates, and even strangers will often ask questions. Leslie recalls, ''The kids at school and in the neighborhood would bother Gary when he was five and six. Sometimes they were just curious. They constantly asked him, 'Is that your mother?' It went on all the time.''

Gary remembers those incidents, too. ''The schools I went to always had lots of black students, and most of my friends were black. They would ask me about my mom because she was white, and I would say, 'Yes, that's my mom all right.' They would ask, 'How come, man?' and I would tell them I was adopted. It bothered me at first, but I grew out of that. It is hard to explain adoption.''

Leslie's last name was Irish when Gary was in elementary school. He recalls that on the first day of school each September ''when my name was called in class, the teachers and kids would look around and expect someone white. When they saw me, they were surprised. They'd say, 'That's you?' or they would come up to me and ask, 'Why do you have a name like that?' and I would explain if I wanted to. Later, when my mother married, my father adopted me, and my last name was no longer noticeable.''

BLACK IDENTITY

The development of a sense of self is complicated for an adopted child whose parent is of a different race. The black child feels related to the white parent, and thus a black child will feel in some measure white. This child needs to develop an identity as a black person. This is difficult if the family lives in an all-white community. The black child may not see black adults or any other black children.

In the process of growing, children identify with those around them. Black children in all-white communities have little choice but to identify with white people. In a race-conscious society, they will be confused about who they really are. This confusion can be worsened if white members of the family pretend that everyone in the family is the same and that no differences exist among them.

Leslie Lewis had thought this issue through before she adopted Gary, and from the time of Gary's adoption, the family lived in an integrated neighborhood that was more heavily black than white. "I made a conscious decision to live where I would be in the minority and my children would be in the majority." Thus, the children would have black friends, and would see black teachers and other adults who were black with whom they could identify.

AFRICAN AMERICAN CULTURE

In addition to the importance of identifying with black people, it is important that children be proud of their race. Those who are ashamed of their race will have difficulty feeling good about themselves. Leslie spent much time reading and learning about black history and black culture so that she could pass on the knowledge to Gary and Brian, her second adopted son. "I gave them the history of black culture as I learned it from books," she explains. "We had black history games, comic books, and storybooks. We talked about blacks in history and in the arts and sciences. It was a constant part of our life. For example, when we traveled on the subway, I mentioned that a black engineer, Granville T. Woods, invented the electrified third rail for the subway trains. Wherever we traveled, we visited places important in black history, and we attended dance, music, and culture programs related to black Americans. It was my mission to provide my children with these experiences and this information so they would know their own racial heritage.''

Gary says he had no problems about who he was. ''I knew who I was. I knew I was black, but I associated with both groups—white and black. There were differences, though—small things. All black families knew certain things that I didn't. Most of the kids were Baptist or Presbyterian. They dressed differently and ate different foods. Some kids would come to school wearing different styles. I wondered how they knew about these styles when I didn't. They all had relatives down south. They ate different foods, like chitterlings. I pretended I ate that, too, but I never did. My mother would show us all kinds of different things and serve us different foods. I happened to like quiche. I don't think I acted white. The black kids accepted me. I was tall and played basketball. My brother and I identified with blacks. It was no big deal.''

RACISM

In addition to developing a strong sense of self as a black person, and self-respect and pride in one's black heritage, Leslie knew that another issue had to be faced. There was the danger that racism would cause harm to her black children.

''I always treated race as a front-burner issue. Uncomfortable things often get put on the back burner, but I couldn't allow that. Racism exists. We couldn't pretend it didn't. I told the kids that race would be an everyday issue for our family. They could feel any way they wanted to about it.

''I remember one incident when Gary was still very young—five or six years old. It was summertime, and we had gone to a department store to look for an air conditioner. I was shopping, and Gary was wandering around the aisles. Suddenly there was all this noise behind me. I turned around and saw a manager picking up Gary. They were going to throw Gary out of the store because they didn't know he was with me. They just thought he was a little black kid walking around the store alone.

"In our family we talked about what we called the black kid syndrome. Black kids were often suspected of having done something wrong, and my children had to know how to deal with that. I would say to them, 'I know you don't steal, but some other people may be suspicious of you.' I knew I had to protect them and warn them. I told them, 'You can't do certain things without getting into trouble.'

"They had to learn that a racist society imposes certain restrictions. I said, 'It isn't right,' but I couldn't tell them to go ahead and do what they wanted, because I didn't want them endangered. My kids knew it was out of caring for them that I told them to take care of themselves. Black males especially have to be extremely careful."

Two years after Leslie adopted Gary, she applied to adopt a second child. She believed it was important for Gary to have somebody like himself, and she wanted to expand their family so that the relationship between her and Gary would not become too intense. But this was in 1974, and a major change had occurred in the world of adoption. Transracial adoptions were virtually banned. White parents were no longer permitted to adopt nonwhite children except in extreme situations. The only black children who could possibly be adopted by a white parent were those who were older and troubled and who would never otherwise get a family. When Leslie was able to adopt for a second time, in 1974, it was just such an older, troubled child.

THREE DECADES OF
TRANSRACIAL ADOPTION

THE WORTHS

"Anna and I adopted Nkomo in 1966 when I was a graduate student in history at Louisiana State University. At the time I was deeply involved in the civil rights movement in the South," explains David Worth.

When the Worths, who are white, adopted their infant African American daughter, they already had three young biological sons. Although white parents adopting a black child had been essentially unheard of before the 1960s, the new spirit of the civil rights movement was altering many people's ideas about racial distinctions between black and white.

"A group of students from Louisiana State had joined the civil rights sit-in protests at lunch counters in Mississippi. The sit-ins were organized by the Student Nonviolent Coordinating Committee," David continues. "I was older than most of the other students, and was already married with three young sons, when I went with the group. We also went from door to door registering black people to vote."

Since Anna was caring for the three young Worth children at the time, she could not participate as much as her husband, but she also supported the civil rights movement. Around her in the Louisiana community, she could see the unfair treatment that black people endured daily because of segregation laws.

Among the many people the Worths met in the civil rights movement in the South were some child-welfare workers. From them they learned of black infants in need of adoption; one was Nkomo.

"At that time there weren't many people clamoring to adopt a six-month-old black child," says David. "We believed that if we did not adopt her, she would grow up in a succession of overcrowded foster homes or in an institution. After three sons we very much wanted a daughter, so we decided to adopt Nkomo. We expected to face criticism, mostly from racists, but that didn't discourage us."

THE ASHLEYS

James and Margaret Ashley had tried unsuccessfully for a number of years to have a child. Finally in 1969 the Ashleys, who are white, chose to adopt Kirk, a black baby boy. The Ashleys live in a small Pennsylvania city surrounded by farms, beautiful countryside, and many lakes. Their home is an old-fashioned farmhouse with an inviting front porch shaded by oak trees. As sometimes happens, two years after they adopted Kirk, Mrs. Ashley gave birth to a son, Frank, and three years later to a daughter, Liz. Two years after the birth of Liz, the couple adopted a black girl, LaToya. They are now a family with four children, two black and two white.

"When we adopted Kirk in 1971," says Mrs. Ashley, "more black children were available for adoption than white children, and we just wanted a kid."

CHANGING TIMES

The Ashleys and the Worths were affected by the major change that had taken place in the world of adoption. Transracial adoptions had been rare before 1960, but by 1971, one-third of all black children being adopted were placed with white families. By 1972 approximately 20,000 black children had been adopted by white families.[1] This extraordinary change resulted from the convergence of two unrelated events: the change in birth control practices, and the new attitudes produced by the civil rights movement.

Because of the legalization of abortion in 1973 and the introduction of the birth control pill in the 1960s, fewer women were having unwanted babies. As a result, there were more white couples who wanted to adopt babies than there were white babies available for adoption. No doubt many couples seeking to adopt a white baby would not have considered adopting a nonwhite child. There were, however, some couples, like the Ashleys, who would adopt a black child because they "just wanted a kid."

Some couples, like the Worths, were able to have biological children, but also wished to add to their family and provide a home for a black child. The Worths and other couples had been deeply affected by the civil rights movement led by Dr. Martin Luther King, Jr., and others. They believed that their adoption of needy black children was a good deed and would also move America closer to true integration.

Some couples who were unable to have biological children sought to adopt black infants when they found there were few white infants available for adoption. The civil rights movement, by changing attitudes about racial segregation and by fostering a spirit of integration, made it possible for white people to adopt black children.

In 1968, affirming the new climate, the Child Welfare League, an organization concerned with public policy, reversed its long-standing opposition to transracial adoption and stated that it was no longer necessary to match the race of parents and children in adoption.[2]

THE ROLE OF THE ADOPTION AGENCIES

Ruth McRoy, an author and researcher in the area of adoption, claimed at a North American Council on Adoptable Children (NACAC) conference in 1990 that the adoption agencies had discriminated against black people by making it difficult for them to adopt. With many fewer white babies to place, these agencies developed more stringent requirements for adoptive parents: a couple had to be infertile and younger than thirty-five, and its income had to be above a certain level. Waiting lists of prospective adoptive parents were established, and the adoption agencies increased the fees charged for their services. This reduced the number of applications from black adoptive parents. Agencies became more willing to allow adoption of nonwhite babies by white families because few white babies were available for adoption. McRoy charges that these agencies were more concerned with the needs of their white clients than with the needs of the black infants. Instead of seeking out black adoptive parents, the social workers placed black babies with white families.

On the other side, however, are those who claim that even if the adoption workers had worked zealously to find black couples, there would not have been enough couples to adopt all the black children who were waiting.

HARD-TO-PLACE CATEGORY

The category of "hard to place" developed at this time. Since the agencies had difficulty placing black babies with black parents, the adoption workers described the black infants as "hard to place." Such a category suggests that few people want the child because there is something wrong with the child, but critics say the agencies' strict requirements and inadequate recruitment are at fault.

THE REACTION OF THE 1970s

In 1972 in St. Louis the main address at the conference of the North American Council on Adoptable Children (NACAC) was delivered by the president of the National Association of Black Social Workers. Among the adoption advocates and adoptive parents attending were many white couples who had recently adopted black babies. The unexpected statements of the keynote speaker devastated the audience. He accused white parents who had adopted black babies of committing cultural genocide. "Their children," he charged, "wouldn't develop black pride and a black identity, both of which they sorely needed to grapple with society and racism."[3]

"There was incredible hurt in the crowd," recalls one adoptive mother. "I was in terrible pain." Some parents wept. And a few, fearful they would destroy their babies' lives, gave them back to adoption agencies.[4]

The National Association of Black Social Workers (NABSW), a group with 5,000 members, had dramatically announced its position. The association objected to the transracial adoptions of the 1960s and introduced a conference resolution opposing all such adoptions. The response in the adoption field was swift. Almost immediately nearly all transracial placements ceased.

How could a practice that had been viewed as well intentioned and generous suddenly be regarded as cultural genocide? What led the association of black social workers to denounce transracial adoptions?

In the early days of the civil rights movement people assumed they were building a truly integrated society. Social workers were routinely placing nonwhite babies with white couples, believing that skin color was not a central issue. Thus the social workers' strong criticism of transracial adoptions was very disturbing.

As the philosophy of the 1960s civil rights movement began to give way to a rising sense of black nationalism, the issue of being black in America became more heavily publicized. Phrases such as "Black is beautiful" and "Black Power" echoed the new feeling. The early civil rights movement had encouraged integration and fostered a belief in transracial adoption. With the shifts in thinking coming from the Black Power movement, attitudes changed, and attention was focused on the need to be proud of being black. As part of the new emphasis, black social workers began to question how black children in a white family could develop strong black identities. Would black children raised in a white family always feel inadequate because they were not white?

In 1968 the Child Welfare League took a position in favor of transracial adoptions, but in 1973 the group reversed its stand and issued a ban on transracial adoptions. In 1978 the Indian Child Welfare act was passed. This law required that Indian children remain wards of the tribal council and not be adopted by white parents.[5]

With these changes in attitudes, the adoption of black children by white parents virtually ended in the 1970s. When such placements did occur, the adoptees were older children.

In the 1970s and 1980s many transracial adoptive families became keenly aware through their own experiences that racial identity and racial background were of the utmost significance for their adopted children. The transracial families began to look for books about African Americans and to seek contact with African American families and organizations so that their children would not be surrounded by just white people. Some families moved into more integrated communities and made certain their children attended integrated schools.

TRANSRACIAL ADOPTION IN THE 1980s

In the 1980s the ban on transracial adoptions was challenged in the courts. The American Civil Liberties Union (ACLU) sued in several states on behalf of white parents who had been denied an adoption of a nonwhite child. The ACLU charged that the parents were being discriminated against on the basis of race. In every case the courts ruled that race could not be the most important consideration in an adoption. However, these court rulings have not had much effect outside the courtroom on the practices of adoption agencies. Indeed, thirty-five states still have restrictions on transracial adoptions.[6]

The annual conference in 1972 of the North American Council on Adoptable Children was the occasion of the first resolution opposing transracial adoption. Since then the council has periodically addressed this difficult issue through a series of policy statements. In 1981 the NACAC board stated that, ''while supporting same race placement, [it] acknowledged that some children may need to be placed transracially rather than continue to wait in foster care.''[7]

In 1988, sixteen years after the first objections to transracial adoption, Sydney Duncan, a black woman and founder of Homes for Black Children in Detroit, addressed the NACAC's annual conference. In her speech entitled ''Healing Old Wounds,'' she stated the problems involved in transracial adoption and offered suggestions. ''The past sixteen years of struggle about the rightness of transracial adoptions resulted in some positive service gains for Black children; at the same time, it has also caused considerable pain and anguish for all of us within the adoption community. . . . For those of us who are Black, the pain has been fear of losing control of our own destiny through loss of our own children. For those of you who are white and have adopted transracially, the pain has been denial of your right to parent a child that you have accepted into your family and call your own." Ms. Duncan asked of those in the adoption community, both black and white, "How do we help each other?"[8]

She went on to say, "For those of you who are white . . . I believe we as Black people can be of help . . . as you seek to give your children of color answers about their heritage. And answers about the craziness of our world in relation to color. And as you seek to give them answers to questions for which every adopted child seeks answers.

"For those of you who are white I ask help and moral support as we Black people seek to mobilize the mainstream of Black families, that unknown majority within our community that I believe has the capacity to respond to the vast numbers of Black children who are entering the system."[9]

ADOPTION IN THE 1990s

The 1990s present yet another situation. We have acquired much new information in recent years, not just about transracial adoption but about adoption in general and about the problems adopted children must face.

At the same time the problem of parentless children has reached crisis proportions. Thousands of minority children are languishing in foster care rather than growing up in permanent adoptive homes. Many people claim that the adoption system is in need of reform because it is not serving the needs of the children. Consequently the issue of transracial adoption must be given full attention again.

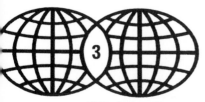

SEAN MURPHY:
A BIRACIAL IDENTITY

Sean Murphy was adopted in 1972 at the age of five months. His white adoptive father says that from the time Sean was a small child in nursery school, he was comfortable about his race and exhibited self-confidence.

"I remember when he was four or five," says his father, "one of the kids in nursery school was criticizing Sean for being dirty, and Sean went to the teacher and said, 'Please tell that kid I'm not dirty, I'm black.' He came home from school and told us about it. I was real pleased. It showed he was comfortable being black, and he was comfortable standing up for himself in the classroom. It was an all-around positive sign."

Sean had shown that he had strong self-esteem, was proud of being black, and knew that the problem lay with the other child, not with himself. This was a major accomplishment for him.

After the birth of their first biological child, the Murphys were told that they could not have a second child. Thus, when their daughter was three years old, the Murphys applied to adopt a baby. (Eventually, the Murphys did have another biological child, Dierdre, who is five years younger than Sean.) At the time of their application to adopt, the Murphys told the social worker that they would be able to raise a nonwhite child.

Sean Murphy was born in 1971 to an Irish Catholic woman and an African American man. Sean's biological mother had stipulated to the adoption agency that he be raised in a Roman Catholic family.

At the time of his adoption, Sean was considered biracial rather than black or white, because his biological mother was white and his father was black. The agency could place Sean with a white couple, since he was half white.

Shortly after Sean's adoption, however, black activists began to question the designation of these children as biracial. Since society regards these children as black, they claimed, the agencies were fostering an illusion by claiming that such children were biracial. Eventually agencies stopped classifying as biracial the children of one black and one white biological parent. These children were considered African American and were no longer placed with white adoptive parents.

Although Sean is of biracial background, he is considered nonwhite by an institutionally racist society. The activists are correct in saying that society regards and treats these children as black. The issues are the same for Sean as for a black child: coping with racism, building self-esteem when treated as an inferior person, developing pride in a racial and cultural background, developing an individual identity as a nonwhite person. At the same time, Sean considers himself an interracial person.

THE NEIGHBORHOOD

The Murphys had expected to wait at least a year before they would be able to adopt. However, since Sean's mother had specified that he be placed in a Roman Catholic home, the Murphys, who are Roman Catholics, jumped to the top of the waiting list. In a short time, by February 1972, five-month-old Sean was placed with the Murphys. Until his adoption the infant had lived in foster homes.

"I went into this wearing rose-colored glasses," Karen Murphy admits. "I thought all you needed to do was give the kid love. But that's not always the case."

Rose-colored glasses or not, the Murphys realized that having an interracial family would be difficult in the neighborhood in which they were living. The Murphys chose to move away from their city home to a small town, where they felt that people would not be so prejudiced against their adopted child. Their community consists of 150 houses set amid pine trees on the shore of a lake. In the surrounding area, which is rural and yet suburban, there are lovely homes, spacious lawns, and picture-postcard villages. The families living in the nearby towns are financially comfortable; many could be called rich.

"We picked this community because it was unusually tolerant," Karen explains. "People who live here are affluent, but status is not all-important. They live here because they like the outdoors and want their privacy." The community is almost all white, but Karen says that "overt racial prejudice would be considered bad form. People here are too polite for that, if nothing else." Sean himself does not recall any incidents of racism.

His father believes that Sean has always had a good self-image, perhaps in part because people's response to him has always been so positive. "The families here all live around the lake and belong to the beach club. In the summer Sean would be at the beach every day, and very quickly everybody got to know him," his father recalls. "From the time he was a little boy people always fussed over him."

High self-esteem is essential to all children as they are growing up, but if they are treated in a racist manner, their self-esteem can easily be damaged. Racists treat nonwhite children as inferiors, and the danger is that the children may wonder if the racists are right and if they really are inferior. Of course, nonwhite children raised in black families can be affected by racism just like children in transracial homes. Critics of transracial adoption say, however, that white families may ignore the problems of racism or not know how to help the children protect themselves. It seems fortunate that the Murphys moved to a community where people accepted Sean.

His father says he started talking to Sean about racism when he was still very young: "I tried to tell him there would be people who wouldn't like him because of the color of his skin. I did this when he was three or four or five years old. It wouldn't do any harm to start early, I thought, and the information would be there when he needed it. I told him to try not to take it personally, that they were ignorant people because they chose to be ignorant."

BIRACIAL IDENTITY

Despite the argument that these children should not be considered biracial, Sean sees himself as being of both races. "My biological mother was blond, and my biological father was a crispy black, so I'm halfway, a mix," he says. "I don't have a black personality, and I don't have a white personality. I'm a blend of the two."

Sean appears to embrace both sides of his racial and cultural background, and he refuses to let society define him. "I'm not one to be put in a box," he says. "I'm big on being unique. I can't be just one or the other, just black or just white, due to my background. I am genetically both. Both sides complement each other. For a while my hairstyle was a high-top fade—six inches high. Dierdre, my little sister, tells me that in church I stand out. She thinks it's cool but that maybe I shouldn't stand out so much. But I'm not going to conform. If it's in me it has to come out. Now I wear dreadlocks on the top of my head, and the side is shaved, and I wear an earring in my left ear. Dierdre thinks it's hip. My parents always ask me, when am I going to cut my hair. My father jokes with me and warns me to lock my bedroom door at night or he'll come in while I'm asleep and cut my hair.''

Sean's musical interests reveal his creativity, his enjoyment of self-expression, and a blending of cultures. In junior high he had his own band, and he played tenor saxophone in the high school band. ''I like all good music, not just one kind of music. I listen to reggae and hip-hop and jazz. I have Bob Marley and Paul Simon in the same collection.''

AN AFRICAN AMERICAN BACKGROUND

The Murphys were attentive to Sean's African American heritage, and they made sure he learned African American history. Although he grew up in a white area, he received a background in black culture. Sean's father recalls, ''As Sean was growing up, Karen would pick up books about black historical figures. There was a set of biographies of historical figures that were like classic comic books, and Sean loved them. They were among his favorite things.

''Karen did other things as well. She bought one of our daughters a black doll. It was a very nice doll, and it was not one of those dolls that are brown in color but have white features. It had black features.

''We also tried to keep Sean in touch with other nonwhite people. For a while he was the only black kid in his grade school, but most of the time he had contacts with other nonwhite people. I have a cousin who married a Puerto Rican man, and together they adopted Mexican and Colombian kids. And Sean's grandfather's neighbors were an Indian family.''

FRIENDSHIPS

Sean's parents note that people of all races like and accept Sean. His father says, ''Sean is a great kid. He's a kind person, a nice person. And he's always been good-looking and sociable.''

"His charm and his sympathetic manner make him accepted everywhere," says his mother. "Maybe it's because he's always been different that he's so accepting of other people." People in turn, like him, she says. "No matter where he's put, he fits in. He's always been comfortable with his color and who he is."

But there were problems during his youth. The first time Sean went away to summer camp, he found it harder to mix with the black kids than with the white kids. "That was because I had always been around white people up until then," he explains. But eventually he learned to get on with both groups, he says. "Half of my friends are white and half are black," Sean says. "I feel accepted by both."

Some young black people who have grown up in white families have felt rejected by other black people, some of whom accuse them of "acting white." But Sean says that black young men accept him as one of them. "Black guys accept me. Being black is your personality as well as your race. Black guys take me for black, but black girls see me as exotic. White girls see me as exotic, too."

A black classmate who was on the junior high track team with Sean once said to him, "Why don't you get your own color?" This probably was a reference to Sean's acting more like the white people in his community.

AN INTERRACIAL FAMILY

"I didn't question the color difference in my family," Sean says. "I accepted it. I didn't feel out of place. I never longed to be what I wasn't. The difference between me and my parents gives me a wider view. I can see things from both the black and the white perspective."

Sean goes on to say, "My older sister Jenny and I did not get along. I was always trying to figure her out. When she hurt me, my dad would talk about it with me. I came in as a baby when she was three years old, and the difference made me seem special. The race difference was not the number one cause, but it had a definite part in the problems between us."

Karen Murphy says that Sean always got a great deal of attention because he was an adorable baby, and she thinks that Jenny resented this deeply.

"Dierdre looks up to me as her older brother," remarks Sean. "We have a good relationship. She thinks my hairstyle, for example, is wild, cool, but she appreciates it and says it looks good on me."

BEING ADOPTED

"Being interracial, I couldn't hide from being adopted," Sean explains. From the time he was very young, his parents told him he was adopted, but he didn't ask questions until later. "I think when I was six or so, I had questions as to why. I pretty much accepted it. My biological parents made the decision that was best. My biological mother wanted a Catholic family and a strong family structure, so she wanted me to have what she thought was best for me. It's not sad for me to talk about it at all. But my friends would have a complex about it when they first met my parents. They wouldn't expect to see these were my parents.

"My family would go to the adoptive family group picnics, but I felt out of place at them. I felt I wasn't adopted. I felt adjusted. Being adopted is a big thing and it's not to be taken lightly, but I was doing okay. That group wasn't for me."

Sean does not want to meet his biological parents. "I have parents already," he says. "I have a family." He says he would like to watch his biological parents as they went about their daily lives, without actually meeting them. "I might sit outside the A&P and watch my biological mother shop. I would be curious.'' But he wonders how they would feel about it. ''What would I do if a young man came up to me and said 'I'm your son'?'' he asks.

''I can only speculate about what my life would have been had I not been adopted. My background has shaped my life, but I'm going in my own direction now.''

REFLECTIONS ON THE FAMILY EXPERIENCE

What advice would Karen Murphy give other parents considering adopting a child of a different race? ''Be sure that your parenting skills are good and that your family is intact. If there are problems in your marriage, it will be hard to fulfill someone else's needs. And be prepared for the issues that will be raised around the abandonment of the child by the biological parent. Underneath, the adopted child feels rage at this.''

On reflection she wonders whether she and her husband made the correct choice of a place to live: ''I wonder if it wasn't unfair of me to raise Sean in a white neighborhood. In a way, it may be pure luck that he had a charming personality that enabled him to get on well with everyone. I did what was easier for me; I wanted to live in the country by a lake. As a result, I kind of put him in a cocoon.''

Whatever problems Sean may have, his mother attributes primarily to the wound of abandonment. The difficulty stems from the initial rejection by the birth parents, she maintains, and not in the difference of race in the adopted family.

THE PROCESS OF ADOPTION

In the United States there are private adoption agencies, often funded by religious and philanthropic groups, and public adoption agencies funded by city, state, and federal taxes. Public adoption agencies are administered by city or state governments; private adoption agencies are run by private individuals or organizations. Adoptions arranged by agencies, public or private, are called public adoptions. Adoptions not arranged through an adoption agency are referred to as private adoptions.

A private adoption is also sometimes called an independent adoption, or an identified adoption. No adoption agency is involved. The adoptive parents receive the child through direct contact with the birth parent. Lawyers and sometimes doctors often serve as intermediaries in these adoptions. After the adoptive parents receive the child, they petition the court for permission to adopt. The court requires that a social worker perform a home study of the family just as in an agency adoption.

When the Murphys applied to a private Catholic adoption agency, their first step was to attend an orientation meeting. During that session they heard about the agency's policies and its requirements for prospective parents, dealing with age and marital status, and the costs that would be involved. After information sessions like this one, people decide if they want to apply to the adoption program.

The Murphys' application included their family biographies, a statement of finances, and medical reports. In addition, they submitted references from Mr. Murphy's employer and character references from several people who were not relatives.

Once an agency accepts this application, a study of the home begins. A social worker interviews the family, visits their home, and evaluates their ability to be adoptive parents. The prospective parents attend several group discussions to prepare them for situations they may face once they adopt a child. Through these sessions, they are also introduced to a network of other adoptive families.

Descriptions of these meetings by the social worker become the home study report, which the adoption committee approves or rejects. Once approval has been granted, a waiting period ensues. When a child is available for whom this couple seems suited, the placement occurs and the child moves into the adoptive parents' home.

This waiting period before placement in the adoptive home varies greatly. A newborn infant can be placed in a home immediately after birth. On the other hand, children adopted from foreign countries are generally not placed immediately. In some cases, the adoptive parents travel to the foreign country to bring the child home. Children adopted from countries such as Korea travel by plane with an adoption worker and are met at the airport by their adoptive family. An older child, perhaps of school age, adopted from within the United States, may need many visits over an extended period of time to become comfortable with the new family before moving into the adoptive home.

An adoption supervision period traditionally lasts for six to twelve months after the adoption. During this time the social worker meets regularly with the child and family to assist their adjustment. In the last step of the adoption process the court formalizes the placement with a judgment decree.

Adoption is a complex process aimed at creating a family. Children cannot be purchased or randomly chosen. Agencies and the courts must ensure that the best possible family is found to meet the individual needs of each child.

THE ADOPTION
CONTROVERSY

"We strongly believe Blacks should adopt Black children, and if provided an opportunity to do so, they will. Our position is that the African American family should be maintained and its integrity preserved. We see the lateral transfer of Black children to White families as contradictory to our preservation efforts," said Dr. Morris Jeff, president of the National Association of Black Social Workers (NABSW), in 1987 in an article in *Ebony* magazine.[1]

The NABSW maintains that black children who are adopted by white families are robbed of their racial identity, prevented from developing the coping mechanisms they need to function in a racist society, and consequently experience serious psychological problems during adolescence and adulthood.[2]

In this controversy the black social workers have been among the most vocal in their objections to transracial adoptions. Other observers strongly disagree with the NABSW's position.

The researchers of the most comprehensive study of transracially adopted children, Rita James Simon and Howard Altstein, dispute the accusations of serious psychological problems. "To this date [1988], no data have been presented that support the belief that in the long run transracial adoption is detrimental to those involved. On the contrary, evidence . . . indicates positive results."[3] Nevertheless, the researchers say, "A belief that transracial adoption is unnatural and therefore bound to be unsuccessful continues to be popular among many child-welfare professionals."

BARRIERS TO ADOPTION BY BLACK FAMILIES

Many adoption advocates believe that rather than agitating against the adoption of black children by white families, the focus of concern should be on lifting the barriers against black families who seek to adopt. Observers point out that numerous black people who would consider adopting are not being reached by the foster care and adoption agencies. In their study of nonwhite children in white families, Simon and Altstein support this view. "Black people have not adopted because child-welfare agencies have not actively recruited in black communities using community resources, the black media, and the churches."[4]

Leora Neal, director of the NABSW's adoption service, has said, "Many adoption officials believe there aren't enough black families willing to adopt. We know that's not true. There are thousands of blacks who are willing and able to adopt black children, but particularly those who are single, over forty, and with modest incomes are often met with discouragement and discrimination from mostly white social workers who know little about black culture and the black community."[5]

According to many specialists, various practices of the agencies discourage black families, as for example, adoption fees that are often beyond the means of black potential parents with lower incomes. Subsidies given to black adoptive parents would help to defray the costs of an adoption.

Another reason fewer black children are adopted lies in the barriers to adoption within the foster care and adoption system itself. Some of the barriers to adoption stem from laws governing the findings of child neglect and abandonment, termination of parental rights, and the freeing of a child for adoption. These laws, combined with overcrowded court calendars and understaffed courts and welfare agencies, cause delays—sometimes of years—in the adoption process. The time and the legal wrangling involved discourage adoptions. In addition, social workers with too many children to supervise may neglect to push for adoption of a foster child.

If there are not enough black homes for black children it is not because black families do not adopt. Quite the contrary. They do so in greater numbers than other groups. Proportionately, more black people than white people give homes to children who are not their biological children. This includes not only formal adoption but kinship care and other informal child-rearing arrangements.

BLACK FAMILY RECRUITMENT PROGRAMS

Some black adoption specialists have developed special programs for finding potential black parents. The Three Rivers Adoption Agency in Pittsburgh, for example, conducts culturally sensitive parent–home studies, according to Azizi Powell, a member of the agency's staff. Some aspects of a culturally sensitive program are: African Americans in administration, the location of the agency in black or integrated communities, the accessibility of staff to the clients, a schedule of evening and Saturday hours, the full sharing of information with clients and advocacy for the clients by the staff.

Another group that makes an effort to find black homes for black children is the One Church, One Child program founded by a Roman Catholic priest in Chicago. Father George Clements, a black priest, has set an example by adopting four black teenage sons. In this program, which has been taken up by many black Protestant churches, each church pledges to find a family within its congregation or its community to adopt a child. The program has located homes for hundreds of black children.

However, even after great efforts have been made to find black families for black children in need, some children's advocates claim there will still be black children waiting for permanent homes.

SUPPORT FOR TRANSRACIAL ADOPTION

Placing black infants in black families is not a problem, according to adoption agencies. This may also be true for children of preschool age. However, there may not be enough black parents interested in adopting children older than three or four. Children more easily form loving attachments when they are adopted at an early age. Should an agency force a child to wait indefinitely for a same-race adoption, or should there be a limit on the time allowed for searching for black parents? Advocates of transracial adoption say that rather than wait for a same-race family that may never be found, one should make a permanent placement in a white adoptive family if one is available.

RESEARCH IN TRANSRACIAL ADOPTION

In the early 1970s, when black children were first adopted by white parents, no one could predict how successful these adoptions would be. Now, twenty years later, those children have grown to adulthood. In the intervening years, studies conducted by social scientists and researchers documented the effects of transracial adoption on all members in the families. The most significant in-depth studies are *Transracial and Inracial Adoptees: The Adolescent Years*, by Ruth McRoy and Louis Zurcher, and *Transracial Adop-*

tees and Their Families, by Rita James Simon and Howard Altstein.

THE McROY AND ZURCHER STUDY

Sixty families who adopted black children were studied; thirty of the parent families were black and thirty were white—an equal number of same-race adoptions and cross-race adoptions. The researchers found similarities between the black parents and the white parents and their adopted black children in several key areas.[6]

• The bonding was strong between parents and children in both the same-race and the transracial adoptive families.

• Black children raised by white adoptive parents had the same high self-esteem and good self-concept as did black children raised by black adoptive parents.

• The black children had close relationships with their brothers and sisters in the family. However, the researchers found that black children did feel closer to other black siblings than to their white siblings.

THE SIMON AND ALTSTEIN STUDY

In late 1971, with the cooperation of the Open Door Society, an organization of adoptive parents, Rita James Simon and Howard Altstein interviewed 204 cross-racial adoptive families living in five states in the Midwest. Each of the families had at least one cross-racial adoption. In all, the researchers interviewed 167 birth children and 199 adopted children. Of the adopted children, 157 were black. The researchers continued the study by revisiting the families at least three different times over a period of twenty years. All the families cooperated with the researchers. "We had an extraordinary response," says Rita Simon, "and that has continued right down to the present with the adult children.[7]

"In 1971 we interviewed adopted children and birth

children . . . between the ages of three and eight," explains Rita Simon. "We interviewed the parents and each of the children separately. We gave the children projective tests about dolls and puzzle pictures of families to see if the children understood the concept of race, if they could accurately identify their own race, and what racial attitudes had already developed among these children.

"Unlike any other data about young black and white children who had been given these same kinds of tests . . . the children showed no preference for one race over another. All the other racial identity studies have shown that both black and white children see white dolls as having more positive characteristics and view black dolls negatively. In our study there was simply no difference. The black and white children chose the dolls randomly; they did not have a preference for either white or black dolls. We found that children who were reared in these kinds of families were growing up color blind. Both the birth children and the adopted children were looking at each other as human beings. Not that he is black but he is my brother, or not that she is white, she is my sister.

"That was a very unusual finding, and when we publicized it, we had some people who said to us, 'Wait until these children get older, all that will change.'

"We also found that among the parents, many of them had not started out with the explicit desire to adopt a black child. They had wanted to give a good home to a child, either because they could not have any of their own . . . or because they felt that it was more humane to adopt than have a biological child, given the number of children in the world who do not have parents. Most of them said they took the first child that was made available to them. When that child turned out to be American black, most of them said, 'Okay, we'll deal with that.' "

The researchers found that no family allowed relatives to discriminate against any of the children. Some of the families joined black churches; others bought books about black culture and black history for their children and themselves.

"Many of the families made some adjustments," Rita Simon says, "but they didn't turn themselves inside out. Most stayed in their own neighborhoods. The children by and large went to integrated schools. Most of them had opportunities for black friends, either through church or school or family friends."

In 1979, when the children were in early adolescence, the researchers returned to the families. They found that one out of four or five of the adopted children was engaged in stealing within the family. They did not steal outside the family. When the researchers consulted psychiatrists they were told that it's not unusual for adopted children to go through some kind of testing, at this age of ten, eleven, or twelve. By 1985 the stealing had stopped. "It was clearly a phase," Simon explains. "There was not one disrupted adoption in all the families we studied."

In 1984 and 1985, when the children were in middle to late adolescence, the researchers returned to the families for a third visit. They gave the children standardized tests that measure self-esteem and integration into the family. The family integration test asks the child questions such as: How happy is this family compared to others? Are you treated the same as your siblings? Do you think your parents understand you?

"On all of these measures we found that there was no difference between the adopted and the birth children," says Rita Simon. "We found that the adopted and the birth children related in the same way to their family. It wasn't smooth sailing," admits Simon. "It never is. But on the whole, the families never attributed these problems to racial differences."

In 1990, twenty years after the adoptions, the researchers again talked to the adopted children and the birth children, who were now adults and no longer living at home.

"We are asking them what is it like," Simon said at that time, "what are their future plans. Some of them are married, and we want to see where they are in their own lives."

The conclusion of the study is that no damaging social or psychological effects on the adopted children were discovered in the transracial families, and that they compared favorably both with the adopted children raised in same-race adoptive families and with the birth children in their own adoptive families. The predictions of low self-esteem and poor self-concept in the adopted children were not borne out. The researchers found that almost all of the parents believed their adopted children had done well and that, if they had not adopted them, the children would have spent their childhoods in institutions or in foster homes.

THE BAN ON TRANSRACIAL ADOPTION

In 1987 Simon and Altstein wrote, "Two decades of research into various aspects of transracial adoption by several investigators in different parts of the United States, using different populations, have for the most part found no adverse effects to any individual or group. Yet despite these findings, stereotypical opposition to transracial adoption seems to prevail at almost all levels of the social service system."[8]

Simon and Altstein clearly state their opinion of a child's need for a permanent family. "We believe that there should be exploration of all permanent and viable same-race opportunities. But where no suitable placement is located, applications from white families seeking to adopt transracially should be examined in as objective and unbiased a manner as possible. We do not believe that same-race foster care placement is preferable to transracial adoption. . . . Adoption, in almost all cases, is a 'forever' placement, whereas the best foster care placement is by definition temporary."[9]

Simon and Altstein point out that transracial adoptions have not been a failure; nevertheless, transracial adoption is not done because child-welfare agencies no longer consider it politically expedient, even though race is not a legally sufficient reason in any state to deny an adoption.

BRIAN LEWIS

In 1974, two years after Leslie Lewis adopted Gary, she applied to adopt a second son. "I didn't want Gary to be an only child," Leslie explains. "He needed somebody like him in the family." But the ban on transracial adoption made only the most difficult to place African American children available for adoption by white parents. Now only a "special needs" child would be placed in a transracial home. As Leslie explains, "It might be a seriously disturbed youngster, much too badly damaged to fit into a family."

Leslie applied to the same agency through which she had adopted Gary, but this time the discussion was not about whom she wanted to adopt but only about whom she would be allowed to adopt. Six months went by before she received a packet with descriptions of three children. Leslie felt that two of them were too old, as they were approaching adolescence. Brian, the third child, was the only possibility. He was listed as a "special needs—hard to place child," and the agency assured Leslie that his problems were emotional. Leslie believed she could handle a child with emotional problems, but should not parent a learning-disabled child.

However, Brian suffered from what is now called attention deficit disorder, and he had profound learning disabilities. In addition, he had spent his first year of life in a hospital and had long-standing medical problems; he had lived eight years in foster care with three different families;

and he had acquired inappropriate sexual experience. A year after his placement in her home, Leslie was still sorting out his special education needs, obtaining medication for hyperactivity, and finding psychotherapy for him.

"After two years, I was ready to admit that I could not manage it with Brian. I asked Gary what he would think if Brian left our home. Gary replied, 'But, Mom, he's my brother.' So that was that. Brian stayed."

Several years after Brian's adoption, Leslie married. John, her husband, is black and also had an adopted son. Together Leslie and John then adopted a three-year-old African American girl. Because Brian's needs were so much greater than those of the other three children, Leslie and John had to give much more to Brian. Their time, attention, and emotional and financial resources were devoted to Brian, sometimes at the expense of the other children.

Brian required years of special programs, residential treatment centers, and therapy. In the end, however, Brian made it. Now twenty-four, he has a steady job, is happily married to a bright and nurturing woman, and has a young son.

"Brian is a survivor," says his mother. "Despite every thing that happened to him in his young life, he survived. If he needed to get to San Diego, I knew I could have given him ten dollars and he would have gotten there."

Under the ban on transracial adoptions, only African American children like Brian, who would never be adopted under ordinary circumstances, could be considered for transracial adoption. Ironically, after 1972, black children like Gary who had only emotional problems, could no longer be placed with a parent like Leslie.

Social workers and child-welfare agencies permitted a ban on transracial adoptions that went against their own professional knowledge of child psychology. Through their training and their experience, these people knew that the children's first and greatest need was for parents who could deal with their needs, nurture and educate them, and help them recover from earlier childhood abuse. Important as racial matching and cultural matching are, they are not as important as a loving home where these children can recover from the abuse, loss, and rejection in their past.

THE ABANDONED CHILDREN

THE CRISIS IN THE CHILD WELFARE SYSTEM

Two-year-old William has been in foster care since birth. His mother, who had HIV infection and was too sick to care for him, died a year and a half after he was born. William is fortunate that he was not born carrying the virus as infants born to HIV-infected mothers sometimes are. Nevertheless, he is one of the thousands of child victims of the AIDS plague now in foster care. HIV infection, drug addiction, and other devastating problems of today's society are contributing to a frightening crisis in the child-welfare system in the United States.

Since the mid-1980s, the number of children in foster care has risen alarmingly each year. In 1991 more than 407,000 children were in foster care, up from 286,000 in 1986, according to Toshio Tatara, director of research for the American Public Welfare Association. The figure may reach 500,000 by 1995.[1] In California, the state with the most children, the number of children in foster care rose 44 percent in the 1980s. On the East Coast, the commissioner of human resources for New York City, Barbara Sabol, reported, "There are now more children in foster care than at any time in our state's history."[2]

The child welfare system was not prepared for this surge in the number of needy children. Barbara Sabol explained the current crisis to a legislative hearing in 1990: "Following the child welfare reform act of 1980, the number of children in foster care dropped dramatically, reaching a low in 1985 of 26,000 in New York State. Then in 1985, the year crack was unleashed, everything changed. Homelessness, drugs, AIDS, and poverty have all affected families. Today 40,000 children are living in foster care in New York City and 60,000 in all New York State."[3]

Adding to the escalating demands on the system, services such as food stamp and child care programs and aid to dependent children that could have helped people were reduced during the Reagan administration. This loss of assistance meant that more parents collapsed under the weight of their problems.

FOSTER CARE IS TEMPORARY

Parentless children are hardly a new problem. For centuries, before the medical advances of modern times, people died at much younger ages and often left behind orphaned children. If there were no family relatives, the children were consigned to orphanages. In the United States in the nineteenth and early twentieth centuries orphanages were overcrowded and highly regimented institutions. Administered by churches or private charities, these orphanages were like warehouses where the abandoned children lived without any semblance of family life. Gradually the child welfare agencies then developed a system of foster homes supervised by child welfare workers. By the 1950s, although some group or institutional care continued for older children, the orphanage had become essentially a thing of the past, replaced by the foster home.

Family foster care was intended to be a temporary solution until an adoption or other permanent arrangement could be made. Unfortunately, the trend today is to leave children permanently in foster care.

The foster care arrangement is best for children who may be able to return home eventually to their family. Many parents have problems that can be remedied in time. Loss of income, homelessness, or eviction can mean that parents find it impossible to keep and care for their children. In other cases emotional problems, such as a depression, make it temporarily impossible for a parent to get out of bed, go to work, make dinner, or do the laundry. These are not necessarily permanent problems. A new job, a rent subsidy, or other help can end homelessness; depressive illness can be treated. It is best to help a family without removing the child from the home. However, if a child must be placed in foster care, the hope is that the family will soon be reunited. In these cases, foster care can actually help families stay together in the long run.

Unfortunately some family situations can never be remedied. Some parents abandon their children at birth; others cannot overcome drug addiction; still others suffer from incurable mental illnesses. These parents may be too sick to take care of themselves, and some of them may constitute a perpetual danger to their children. Such children need more than temporary foster care.

In the past, some foster children who were never able to return to their parents were fortunate to live with one foster family until they were grown. Many children were not so fortunate, however; unable to remain in one family, they were moved numerous times from one foster home to another. For children who experienced such multiple placements, the system was not working.

THE NEED FOR PERMANENCE

Child psychologists recognize that children need the security of a loving and permanent home. Without a permanent family to cherish them, children's self-esteem may be severely damaged; they may conclude that no one wants to keep them because they are worthless. Child-care professionals, having learned this, became concerned by the number of children who were growing up in a succession of foster homes.

Marilyn Monroe, the movie star of the 1950s, is a famous example of a foster child who despite worldwide acclaim was never able to believe in her own value. Marilyn's mother had been in and out of mental hospitals, and her father had abandoned them both soon after Marilyn's birth. The child-welfare agency in Los Angeles removed Marilyn from her mother's home and placed her with a series of foster parents until she married at age seventeen.

Although Marilyn Monroe went on to become one of the most celebrated movie stars of her generation, she suffered from a profound lack of self-esteem, and she never trusted in her own success. In 1965, at the age of thirty-six, she apparently committed suicide. Many of her admirers blame her unhappy childhood for her tragic insecurity and early death.

THE 1980 REFORM OF ADOPTION LAWS

By the 1970s, many children's advocates wanted to reform the child-welfare system. The activists argued that a child should either be returned to the biological family or be freed for adoption. As a result of nationwide pressure, the Adoption Assistance and Child Welfare Act was passed in 1980.

Walter Mondale, then vice president and a longtime advocate for children in the Senate, explained the reasons for signing the law: "What propelled us into action at that time were the many individuals and organizations alarmed by the status of children living in foster care. As chairman of the U.S. Senate Subcommittee on Children and Youth, I held many hearings to review the foster care system.

"What we found was both sad and shocking. An estimated 500,000 children had been removed from their homes and placed in foster care because of abuse or neglect. Yet no one knew how long they had been in the foster care system or what type of effort was being made to find them permanent homes. The adoption assistance and child welfare amendments of 1980 changed all this.

"Our goals were simple and made good sense: (1) keep families together whenever possible, providing them with the services and supports they need, and (2) find permanent adoptive homes for children who could not be reunited with their parents. The Adoption Assistance and Child Welfare Amendments of 1980 were not so simple to implement, however."[4]

The 1980 child welfare act is aimed at shortening the length of time children spend in foster homes. It allows eighteen months in which to restore the biological family and permit the child to return home. If this cannot be done, then the other step—that of adoption—must be taken.

At first the reform seemed to be succeeding. The number of children in foster care declined between 1981 and 1984. But then this trend reversed itself, and the number of foster children began to climb each year until there were more children than the public or private agencies could handle. Ironically, far more children were in the child-welfare system in 1990 than at the time of the reform in 1980. And while the number of children in temporary care is up, the number of adoptions is down. Children are not returning home, and they are not being adopted. In 1990 over 36,000 of the 276,000 children in foster care throughout the United States were awaiting adoption.[5]

ADOPTION OF MINORITY CHILDREN

The majority of the children in foster care are white, reflecting the racial composition of the nation. However, of the approximately 36,000 awaiting adoption, half are nonwhite. While African Americans make up 12 percent of the population, almost 50 percent of the children awaiting adoption are members of minority groups.[6]

Studies show that nonwhite children remain in foster care longer and must wait longer for the completion of the adoption process. For example, in New York City, with its high proportion of minority children, only one out of eight children in need of adoption was actually adopted in 1989. New York Commissioner Sabol points out, "The number of foster children doubled in New York from 1985 to 1990, but the number of public adoptions has decreased. There was in 1990 a 28 percent increase over the previous year in the number of children needing adoption. Despite the increase in the number of adoptable children over the previous year, fewer children were adopted."[7] The decline in the number of adoptions constitutes a crisis in the child-welfare system.

What is stopping the adoptions? State Senator Mary Goodhue of New York has stated, "More than one out of six children who should be moved into the adoptive process remain in the custody of the state . . . as a result of . . . barriers within the system."[8] Commissioner Sabol stated that there has been "a system-wide inattention to adoption in recent years."[9]

Both Goodhue and Sabol direct attention to the child-welfare systems. They argue that something is not working within the system of adoption and that much more must be done to encourage adoptions.

OTHER FACTORS AFFECTING ADOPTION

Many of the 36,000 children awaiting adoption in the United States are over six, the age at which a child becomes harder to place. During the long, slow process of being freed for adoption, some children, ironically, become less adoptable due to their age.

There are also children with special needs, who may have physical handicaps or deformities, neurological conditions, retardation, or complex emotional problems. When an adoptive family is being sought, older children and emotionally troubled children who are not necessarily difficult to parent should not be considered in the same category as children who have more severe disabilities.

TRANSRACIAL ADOPTION AND THE CHILD-WELFARE CRISIS

Twenty years ago, when transracial adoptions first began, some parents did not appreciate the significance of the difference in race between themselves and their adopted children. As long as there is love in a family, skin color doesn't matter, they reasoned. Love is certainly essential to a happy family; however, people have learned that successful transracial adoption also requires a recognition of the unique experiences of the child. As their adopted children grew to adulthood, the families came to understand and found ways to meet the special needs of their black children. The families learned that sensitivity to the importance of racial identity is critical. And, they also discovered that the most pressing task for the child is to come to terms with the loss of the biological parent. This is true for a white child who is adopted into a white family as well as for an African American child adopted into a white family. All adopted children, whatever their race, ask the same fundamental question: Why did my parents give me up? Primarily the child needs an adoptive family that is able to cope with this powerful issue rather than suppress it.

It has also been learned that the younger the child is at the time of the adoption, the better the chance of a good adjustment. This is true whether an adoption is same-race or cross-race. If a white family is sensitive to a five-year-old black child's need in regard to race, should that family be permitted to adopt the child? Or should the child be made to wait until the age of nine or twelve, at which point neither a black nor a white family will be there to adopt?

This is the dilemma of contemporary adoption. The number of abandoned or abused young children is rising at a frightening pace, almost doubling in some areas over a five-year period, and the number of potential parents seeking children is also on the rise. Can the children who need adoptive families be matched with parents seeking to adopt?

SCENES FROM THE LIVES OF TRANSRACIAL FAMILIES

The Simns family

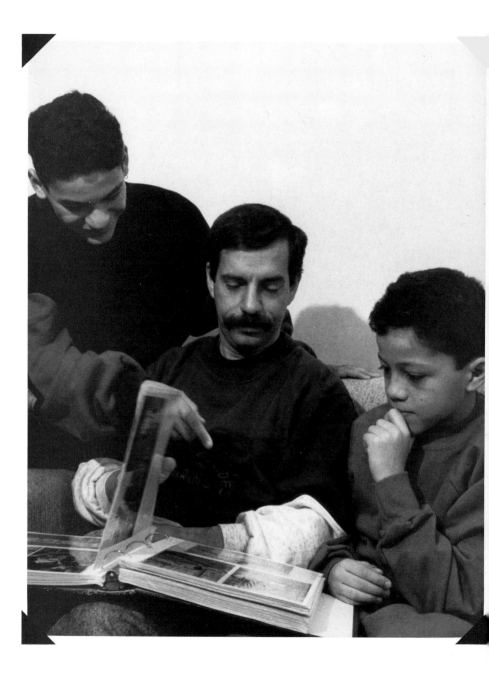

The Cohen family

The Murphy family
(then and now)

**The James family
(then and now)**

The Adams family (then and now)

**The Lewis family
(then and now)**

The Goodman family

THE ADOPTION PROCESS

An adoption-agency social worker (center)
meets with prospective adoptive parents.

Prospective parents with the
child they hope to adopt

At a post-adoption supervision
meeting, a social worker (left)
works with an adoptive mother.

An adoption-agency social worker
meets with a group of adopted children
to discuss their feelings about adoption.

At holiday parties and gatherings
organized by parents' support
groups, adopted children meet other
children in transracial families.

CONTRASTING
EXPERIENCES

Parents and children have many different experiences in transracial adoptions—some good and some bad. In this chapter, Jody, Cal, Sheila, and Lola, four black young people who were adopted into white families, talk about their situations. Sheila and Lola, who live near Montreal, Canada, provide a Canadian perspective. Cal is originally from Tanzania, Africa; Jody lives in an American suburb.

Jody has been injured by racism, although both she and her mother emphasize that she has survived it. Cal, Sheila, and Lola, on the other hand, have had no problems with racism or with the racial differences in their families. Although no adoption is typical, these experiences are examples of what might develop.

JODY SIMNS

Jody, who is now in college, was born to a white woman and a black man. Although she was given up for adoption at birth, she was not placed with her adoptive mother until she was almost two years old. For the first twenty-two months of her life, Jody lived with a foster mother who at first thought she was white. Unlike Sean Murphy who emphasizes his biracial heritage, Jody identifies herself as black.

"My biological parents had to give me up for adoption," Jody explains. "My biological mother was fifteen, and she wasn't in love. I was placed in a foster home, and the woman was going to keep me. She thought I was white, but as I got older I started getting darker. She would give me baths all the time because I guess she thought I was dirty or something. When she realized that I was black, she didn't want me.

"The adoption agency said they wanted to get me out of that home atmosphere as soon as possible. My adoptive mother-to-be was single, and she had almost given up hope of adopting, and then the agency called her. She came to see me, and two weeks later I moved in with her. She had been planning to move away and take another job; it was to be a big career change for her. Instead, she adopted me and stayed."

Jody's mother says, "The white family was going to adopt her until she turned dark. The woman was very ambivalent. She couldn't handle the dark skin, but she later called to ask if I would give Jody back. In the beginning, Jody hated baths. I think she had been bathed several times a day."

Sadly, this experience with racism was not the last for Jody. When Jody was about to enter seventh grade, she and her mother moved to a suburban community that was mostly white. Before that, they had lived in an integrated neighborhood in a city.

"When we first moved to New Jersey, I faced a lot of prejudice. I had a next-door neighbor who was really prejudiced. Their little boy would write things on my mom's house. I hated moving there. When we lived in the city, I was friends with everyone. The race thing never came to my mind. Now I need to be with black people as well as white people, since so many whites treated me in a racist way."

Jody's mother recalls the experience as well. "The boy painted the side of our garage with an epithet, and he called Jody a nigger. The family wouldn't let Jody run across their lawn when all the other kids did. After he wrote on the garage, I went over there and let them know what I thought of them. In the end, though, the other children on the block continued to play with Jody, and it was this little boy who was isolated, not Jody.

"Jody told other people what I had said to that man next door. It was the right thing to do rather than to ignore it. Jody was just in seventh grade, and she was unable to handle this racism on her own."

Early in high school Jody had another experience with racism. Her mother recalls that "when Jody was about fourteen, her closest friends were two white girls. These three girls did everything together. As they got a little older, boys came into the picture, and some of the boys who began to hang around were black. So one girl's mother didn't want her daughter to be friends with Jody. The woman said that Jody wasn't to come to her house anymore. That was devastating for Jody. These three girls had been inseparable. Jody maintained some contact with the girls, but essentially she had no friends that summer. After that she turned to the black girls at the school. They were all lovely girls who came from nice families. Now she is wary of forming relationships, deep ones, with white people. But she'll get over it when she gets stronger."

Jody and her mother have different opinions about the wisdom of moving to this particular suburban community. "I still have a grudge about being raised in an all-white neighborhood," Jody explains. "I was already raised in a white family. I had a lot of arguments with my mother because she moved. She said that in this town I would receive the best schooling. And that's true, but I think it's not fair to any black person. In an all-white school you're looked upon as a totally different person, an alien. And I had trouble with my schoolwork. I had dyslexia so I was put in a lower grade.''

Jody's mother, however, feels that the move was a trade-off. She put a lot of thought into the selection of a community in which she and her daughter could live. "This is a very mixed, open community with a good proportion of black and Asian people. The black families are from the same economic background as we are. I chose this community because these were the kind of people I wanted Jody to be friends with. I have recommended this town to black people I know. They have moved here, and they love it. There's a rural area surrounding us, with farms, cows, sheep, and clean air, and it's safe. The people who live here are highly educated professionals, and they are also artistic, tolerant, and broad-minded.

"In the city neighborhood where we lived, a much larger proportion of the people were poor and uneducated. The junior high had a bad reputation for drugs, and I could not afford to send her to a private school. Also, Jody is learning-disabled—dyslexic—and I knew she would get much better care here than in the city school. Out here she was practically on a one-to-one basis with the teachers. Jody has a high IQ, but she wrote backwards, and her handwriting and spelling were terrible. In the fourth grade, reading became a problem for her. That was how we discovered that she was dyslexic.''

Like parents and children in many situations, Jody and her mother view the suburban experience from different perspectives. Jody thinks her mother should not have "put me in that kind of predicament. I had to go through so much in high school. She still thinks she did what was best, but she doesn't know about everything that happened. I didn't feel I was accepted by either race, because I had a white mother and I was black.'' She adds, "My mother and I are best friends now, and I turned out fine. I think I'm okay now.''

Jody feels that her confusion about her mother being white while she was black made it hard for her to deal with the fact that she was adopted. "When I was younger, people would ask me, why is your mother white?" At this time Jody was attending school with many black children. "I was embarrassed," she says. "I made up stories about my family. If my mother had been black, I think I would have been able to say I was adopted to other black people, to my friends, and to their parents. My mother bought a children's book titled *Why Am I Adopted?* We read it, but I was still confused.

"All my friends were black, and my mother was white. The stress of the adoption upset me, and that made me take it out on my mother. I became a compulsive liar. I argued with my mother a lot."

Jody says that she felt she was not accepted by either race. "Because I was black I was not accepted by the white race, and because I had a white mother I had to lie about the adoption to black people to feel accepted." Jody apparently felt that black people would reject her for having a white mother.

Perhaps because of this confusion, Jody has made a choice. "I definitely consider myself black. I don't consider myself biracial. Black is what I am and what I want to be. I want to raise my children to be proud of their color. I don't want them to go through what I went through growing up. No one was there to say to me, 'Be proud of your color.' I had to learn that on my own."

As for meeting her birth parents, Jody says, "I think that if my birth mother wanted to know about me, she would have gone out of her way to find me. Maybe I would like to find out who she is before she dies, or before I die. Every time I think about it, I say, 'No, I'm scared.' My birth mother doesn't want to know me, and if I looked for her, I would be hurting my mother. As for my birth father, he probably doesn't even know I exist, or care.

"I should be proud of my mother; she's done so much

for me. I never really appreciated how much she did for me until I started living on my own.''

Jody's mother says, "Jody is now at a college that is 70 percent black. It's a small, nurturing school in Pennsylvania. Jody is gaining confidence in herself now. But I feel bad because she's ignoring the white part of herself; she has just as much white heritage as black. Partly she's afraid because of what she has been through, but that may change once she starts to work in a professional setting and mix with people of all colors.

"As for her black heritage, we have always lived near black families,'' her mother explains. "I thought that would help. We did read stories for black children when she was growing up. There are many more available now than there were then. It was hard to get books that were not racist when Jody was growing up. I remember one book I read to Jody where the witch had long gnarled hands with long fingernails that reached across the page. The witch's hands were black. I noticed one day that every time I read that book and we came to that page, Jody hid her hands behind her back. It made a point to me. The color black is evil in these children's books. That's what black organizations should be fighting against. The slogan 'Black is beautiful' doesn't counteract this association of black with evil. I was able to notice Jody's reaction because I was her mother. But what teacher sitting in a room reading to twenty-five or thirty children will be able to notice when one child puts her hands behind her back?''

Jody is studying education in college now, and hopes to be a teacher for a while and then open a day-care center. "I really love working with young people,'' she says.

Jody's mother says of her decision to create a transracial family, "If you can establish a good relationship and love each other, then you can survive the controversy. Jody and I have had our problems. People still stare at us, but it doesn't matter. We really love each other. If I had not adopted her, she wouldn't have had any life. She would have been moved around in foster care. If you don't try to make your adopted transracial children into something they're not, you'll be all right. If you don't acknowledge that they're black, then you'll have a problem.''

CAL

Cal, originally from Tanzania, Africa, had recently graduated from a private high school at the time of this interview, and is now attending college. Cal was born to black Tanzanian parents living in Oslo, Norway, where his father was a graduate student. One month after his birth, he and his parents returned to Dar es Salaam, the capital of Tanzania, where, a year later, his brother was born. Until he was six years old Cal spoke only Swahili.

Cal's mother held a position connected with the United Nations. She had studied for her master's degree in economics in England and could speak English as well as Swahili. Cal's father was a chemist who worked for the Tanzanian government.

His parents divorced when Cal was four, and Cal moved to London, England, with his mother and brother. From that time on Cal had no contact with his father. ''My mother traveled a lot in her job as commonwealth secretary,'' recalls Cal. ''It was almost like an ambassadorship. She traveled from country to country, representing Tanzania. When we got to England, we started learning to speak English immediately. That was my mother's idea.''

While still in Tanzania, Cal's mother had become friendly with a white couple, James and Laura. Eventually James, an American, and Laura, who is British, returned to the United States, but kept up their friendship with Cal's mother. Since his mother traveled so much, Cal and his brother spent a month and a half of every summer vacation with James and Laura in the United States.

When Cal was thirteen years old and his brother was twelve, their mother died of a brain tumor. In her will she had requested that Cal and his brother be adopted by James and Laura. Cal and his brother had not seen or heard from their father since their parents' divorce nine years earlier, and Cal's mother believed that the best family for her two sons would be her friends Laura and James. Soon after the funeral, Cal and his brother moved to the United States and became part of a transracial adoptive family.

How did Cal feel about this? "Laura and James had been very nice to us, like family. I didn't feel uncomfortable about any of the decisions that were made. I think of them as guardians.

"My mother's directions in her will were that I keep in touch with my African relatives. I have a list of relatives in Africa, but I don't remember any of them. I left at four years of age. I don't know my father, and I don't want to. I have received two letters from him in my lifetime. I don't feel about him as my father. Nevertheless he has sued in America to obtain custody of my brother and me, and three times he has lost his case. I cannot return to Tanzania until I am twenty-one, or else my father will claim custody. I would like to see where my mother is buried; that's the only thing that would draw me back to Africa. I feel I'm starting again in America."

Cal does not think any problems arise from the fact that his adoptive parents are white and he and his brother are black. "They have done the utmost to educate me, and they have made me aware of black issues. They haven't forgotten what color I am, that I am of African background. But I have friends who have been adopted into white families and their color and background have been forgotten. The parents have not encouraged the children or given them a chance to learn about their culture.

"My guardians, on the other hand, share my interests. I was interested in how minorities advance in big companies, so they arranged for me to get information from the Xerox Corporation. My father often gives me articles he finds interesting on this subject.

"In England the racism was much more overt. I have found it a lot easier in the United States. I go to a private school, and I can't stand being around some of the parents, but the students listen to me when I speak and treat me as an equal.

"At our school we had a mascot for the sports team that was racially offensive. It was an Indian. I felt strongly about that. We had a campaign to change the mascot. The school was split down the middle, but people were able to discuss the subject openly.

"I have friends who are black, although my school friends are mostly white. Next year I am going to Georgetown University, which has a very active minority student group, and that's going to be interesting, meeting people from a lot of different backgrounds. I am going to major in African American studies and then go on to graduate school in business. I would like to work in the financial world or in sales in a corporation. I have a lot of aspirations for the future. And I want to take care of my family and my brother.''

CANADIAN TRANSRACIAL ADOPTIONS

Lola, seventeen years old, is Senegalese, and Sheila, also seventeen, is from Bangladesh. The two friends now live in a small town in the Laurentian Hills outside Montreal where they are the only black people. "It's beautiful in winter," they say of their town. "We don't experience racism. And there's no prejudice in the schools. They seem to accept us as we are. There are only white people here. I'm surprised if I see another black person," says one of the girls.

Sheila's French Canadian parents have two biological and two adopted children. Sheila's eighteen-year-old adopted brother is biracial. Sheila was eighteen months old when she was adopted and has been told that her biological father left her at an orphanage in Bangladesh.

Lola's biological mother was from Senegal and emigrated to Canada while she was pregnant. Lola was born in Montreal. She was six weeks old when she was adopted by her single French Canadian mother. There are eight adopted children in Lola's family.

"I want to go back to Senegal to learn about my roots, because I'm curious," says Lola. "I'm different from the people in Senegal, even though I am black, but I would like to visit to see what they are like."

"She wants to find her Prince Charming," teases Sheila. "I want to go back to Bangladesh. I want to help out, be a social worker. And I'd like to travel a lot, so I'd start with my own country."

Would they search for their biological parents while in their country? "There's always a part of you that is mad at them, but there's another part that wants to see what they look like," says Sheila. "There's a hole in you that can never be filled, even though people love you."

"I don't have a hole," replies Lola. "I have the same habits as my adoptive mother. When I answer the phone, I sound like my mother. I just want to see what my biological parents look like. I'm just curious."

"Occasionally, if I'm really sad, I ask myself why can't I be with my real parents," says Sheila.

"I never say that," answers Lola.

"On Mother's Day I buy two flowers, one for my mother, one for my other mom," Sheila says.

"You do? I never do that," retorts Lola. "It's my mother who raised me, and she would do anything for me," explains Lola. "I just want to see what Senegal and the people look like."

"I'm an emotional person. I feel a sense of loss sometimes," concludes Sheila.

On dating, Sheila says that every person is different and she doesn't have strong preferences. She is dating a white boy now. "Sometimes I wonder why he is dating a black girl. I'm just like everyone else otherwise. Is he drawn to me because I'm black? I just wonder.''

Lola says she isn't thinking about dating yet. She is considering a career and wants to be a grade school teacher.

A CHECKERBOARD FAMILY

A desire to be white like their parents is a risk for adopted black children, who may be troubled because they are different from the people who love them. They may be angry that they are not white like the rest of the family and thus may not accept their own color.

Black children can also be confused about their racial identity since they may feel that inside they are really white, like the rest of the family, and that they only look black. Such confusion and feelings about color must be brought out and confronted. The children must accept and value themselves even though they are different from their parents. Problems often surface in adolescence when teenagers feel a pressing need to define themselves.

THE LORENZO FAMILY

Julie Lorenzo recalls that when one of her two adopted black sons was asked in a family therapy session what he

wanted to be when he grew up, he answered, "White."
The Lorenzo family has lived through painful times. One
adopted son had race identity problems, and the other suffered from attachment problems.

"Almost every nonwhite kid I work with who is in a
white adoptive home has prayed at one time or another to
wake up white. What does that indicate but a denial of
culture and a self-hate?" asks Jim Mahoney, a social
worker who works with foster children and adopted children in a mental health center in Spokane, Washington.[1]
According to Mahoney, white parents are unaware of many
experiences of their nonwhite children.

"When this nonwhite kid goes to school, to a shopping
mall, or downtown by himself, he is regarded differently
than he is when he's with his white adoptive family. If you
are a child of color, you have to live with a dual role experience. Many children, when something doesn't feel right
and they are stressed, have no language with which to talk
about their discomfort. So sometimes they will act out this
discomfort in school through poor grades. They may also
hang out with the marginal kids in the class. We adults see
this as conduct disorder or a behavior problem. So the parent must deal with a child's negative feelings before the
child begins to trip up at school."[2]

The Lorenzo family has had the experiences Jim Mahoney describes. There are four adopted children; two girls
of mixed race, Hispanic and white, and two black sons who
were born seven weeks apart and adopted a year apart.
"Why did you guys have to adopt a checkerboard family?"
Mark Lorenzo asked his mother and father in a family therapy session.

In 1974 Robert and Julie Lorenzo adopted their first
child, an infant girl, through a Catholic agency. The Lorenzos were living in a small town in Massachusetts where
Julie was a nurse. As she recalls, "I had an infertility problem, and in 1974 one waited two years to adopt a healthy

white infant. I don't know how long the wait is now. The agency telephoned to say they had a healthy infant of mixed race, white and Hispanic. My husband and I discussed it that evening and decided to accept the child.

"Two years later, in 1976, we applied again to adopt through the same agency, but this time we asked for a boy. Once the adoption agency realizes you are willing to accept a nonwhite child, they approach you about other children. So they told us they had a baby boy who was racially mixed—black and white. I was interested. I didn't care what the color was as long as the child was healthy."

Julie had worked with many nonwhite children when she was in nurses' training. "I helped to start an after-school program for underprivileged children. The Catholic church gave us space in the basement, and the community donated supplies. The nursing school was in a Mississippi River town where there was a lot of poverty, and we had a mix of kids—white, black, and American Indian. I continued working in this center throughout the time I was in training. I liked doing it very much. At the center I was around a lot of black children and their parents. I felt good about nonwhite children."

At first Julie's husband, Robert, was taken by surprise by the proposal. His parents lived in the area, and Robert knew they might be upset about what the neighbors would think of a mixed-race child. But as they had taken the first adoption well, Julie and Bob were optimistic that they would adjust. Julie and Bob went to see the infant and then discussed the adoption. The next day they told the agency they wanted to go ahead.

"I didn't understand what the full impact of a trans-racial adoption would be on everyone," says Julie. "It wasn't a problem for me, so I didn't think it would be for anyone else—but it was. It was also difficult for the kids to some degree."

Mark was adopted in August 1976. The Lorenzos did

not want Mark to be the only black person in the family, so they planned to adopt a second black child eventually. Soon after Mark's adoption, however, the state officials announced plans to discontinue placing black children with white families. The Lorenzos realized they would have to adopt a second black child immediately, or they might never have the opportunity again.

In May 1977 they adopted a second black son, Steven, who was 10 months old at the time. Steven and Mark were, in effect, twins, as they were only seven weeks apart in age. "I didn't realize the ramifications of raising two children who were like twins in age but had very different personalities," Julie recalls now. "The sibling rivalry was there, so they were competing with each other in everything."

Because Mark and Steven were the same age, they always compared themselves to each other. And the two boys were opposites in almost everything. Steven was much more verbal than Mark, but Mark was good at sports. Each boy may have felt inadequate compared to his brother and this comparison could have undermined each brother's self-esteem.

MARK: WHO AM I?

When Mark reached junior high school, two major events occurred at the same time: he transferred to a different school, and his parents divorced.

"Mark's troubles started around the time of the divorce," says Julie. "Mark would act out how he felt, since he wasn't able to talk about it."

"All of a sudden Mark changed," says his brother, Steven. "In seventh grade he started getting bad, and then last year in eighth grade he was really bad. He began drinking, and he started sneaking out of the house at night. Despite this, we still have a good relationship.

"In junior high he got into a bad crowd and did a whole bunch of stuff," Steven explains. "We went to different schools. In my school there wasn't really a bad crowd. In his junior high there was."

Mark disobeyed the rules at home and in school, but most disturbing were his violent rages. At first he broke windows in anger, but he soon progressed to carrying a weapon. At his new school there were some tough and violent gangs. Any student caught with a weapon could be suspended. Mark was suspended many times for fighting in school. Later he was caught carrying a knife at school, and then he was arrested in a downtown store for shoplifting. Mark was in various therapy programs, and the family attended therapy sessions together.

"When Mark reached the eighth grade, the whole thing fell apart," says Julie. "In school everything changed. It became important to know who you were racially, and Mark started getting confused and began hanging out with a gang of nonwhite kids who carried knives."

In his new school Mark didn't fit in with the white group racially, even though these students had the same kind of family background and values as he had. In his confusion and pain, he was drawn into a group of tough, gang-oriented troublemakers.

After Mark was arrested a couple of times, his mother petitioned the judge to place the boy in a program that required him to live at a treatment center. To qualify for the program, Mark had to be registered in the foster care system. The court ordered that he first spend forty-five days in a treatment center where his therapeutic needs could be evaluated. This facility was not locked at night, and one evening Mark ran away. The judge then sent him to another treatment center, which was locked at night. While at this center, Mark made a weapon, which he hid in his room. One day he threatened somebody with it.

"All his pent-up anger was coming out," says his mother. Mark's evaluation indicated that he needed residential treatment—that is, he needed to live in a supervised residence and receive therapy. However, there was a two-month wait before he could enter a residence. The court ordered that Mark be placed in a foster home while he was waiting for an opening. Unfortunately, there was very little structure in that home. Mark did not have to be in until midnight, and he stayed out in the streets and got involved with a group of kids who were using drugs. Finally he was arrested with drugs in his possession, and he was removed from the foster home.

Julie then brought Mark back to live at home while waiting for an opening in the residential treatment program. But Mark had concealed a knife again. One evening he announced that he was going out and when Julie told him he was not allowed to leave the house, he pulled out his knife and threatened to use it on everyone in the family. Julie realized that he was a danger to everyone in the household, including himself. She called the court and told the judge that it was dangerous for Mark to remain at home. Another temporary foster home was found for Mark, this time with more structure, and Mark lived there until he was admitted into the residential treatment center.

"It's hard for me to say how much of a factor the transracial aspect was, how much the divorce, and how much the closeness in age of the two boys," says Julie of Mark's problems. "For a while Mark had a fantasy that his mother was black," says Julie, "that there was a black woman out there who was his mother. But his biological mother was white. We were very open about this and all the facts of his adoption. But he was trying to find someone like himself. I sent him to the agency to speak with the adoption worker, and she gave him as much information as there was in the records. The adoption worker described what his mother looked like."

Mark had many of the disturbing experiences of the nonwhite child in the white family, which the social worker Jim Mahoney described. Strangers were often rude to him. People stared at him and asked personal questions. Mark was uncomfortable about his checkerboard family and was not able to talk about his discomfort.

Racist experiences can exacerbate the problem of identity for the nonwhite child. Mark was rejected by the white students in his school, even though his family background was the same as theirs. If he didn't belong with the white students—because of his skin color—then where did he belong? In joining the gangs, he found acceptance as a nonwhite, and their violent behavior provided him with a model for expressing his confusion and hurt.

Mark has completed two years of school and therapy in a residential treatment center and comes home every other weekend. He seems much happier with himself and his family now. He says, "I think it's really neat that my parents can bring up kids of another color. I never wanted to be white like my mother, but people I knew—white friends—made fun of my mother because she was a different color from me. They treated me with disrespect.

"I asked my mom about my birth mother. I wanted to know what she was like. But I wouldn't want to meet her. I'd let her live her life. She might have other kids. It would be odd for me to show up. It doesn't bother me.

"There was no information about my birth father." Of his adopted father, Mark says, "We get along like a regular father and son.

"I like being adopted. Because you have advantages and disadvantages. The advantages are you have fun with your family. The disadvantages are when you get picked on. Other people make problems.

"I feel good about myself. I feel confident that I'm handling my anger. I'm doing great. I'll be out of there [the residential treatment center] soon."

How does Mark now handle his anger, which in the past caused such trouble? "I talk it out. Rather than give in to anger, I storm off. I get some space first, and then I talk the anger out."

At fifteen Mark is accomplished at sports. "I'm a sports fanatic: baseball, football, hockey, basketball, volleyball." He would like to play ball professionally for a while.

STEVEN: WHO DO I LOVE?

Steven Lorenzo had a different set of problems. His difficulties sprang from the disruptions during his first year of life. He was adopted by the Lorenzos at ten months of age. But before that, he had lived with three different families, and each move had a serious impact on him. As a result, Steven had difficulty forming emotional attachments to people.

In the first year or two of life, the infant bonds to the caregiver, usually the mother, whom the child comes to love and trust. Through bonding with the mother during infancy, human beings develop the capacity to care about other people. Without the bond, the child may not develop this ability to love others.

In his first year Steven never remained with anyone long enough to develop this bond. As soon as he started to become attached to a caregiver—that is, to love and trust someone—he was moved to another home. He learned not to trust people but to distrust them, because every caregiver had abandoned him to a stranger. Steven suffered from what therapists call "attachment disorder," an inability to form emotional ties with people. He was an "unattached child."

"As an infant, Steven rejected me," Julie remembers. "When I picked him up, he would try to get out of my arms. Unlike the other children, he never wanted to be held. I even have pictures showing this—family photos in which

I am holding Steven and he is literally pulling away from me, leaning out away from me.

"He became attached to food rather than to people. He stole snacks from the refrigerator constantly. Even as an infant when he could only crawl, he cruised the kitchen floor looking for food. At this time, I didn't know about lack of attachment. It was only when he was in grade school that I talked to other adoptive parents and learned about attachment disorder. When I heard this behavior described, I recognized it as Steven's behavior.

"In first grade or kindergarten—I can't remember which—he was given an exercise to do. The teacher told the children to draw a circle and then to draw inside the circle a picture of what was most important to them. Steven didn't put any people inside the circle. He drew pictures of food instead. There was a refrigerator and ice cream, I think—all food.''

By the time Steven reached third grade it was clear he was having difficulties. He was transferred to a Catholic private school that was stricter and more structured. At about that time Julie learned that techniques for treating attachment difficulties had been developed by Dr. Foster Cline, a psychiatrist who specialized in treating children with this disorder.

At the Attachment Center at Evergreen, Colorado, founded in 1972, Dr. Cline and a team of therapists work with unattached children. Therapists trained to use his techniques are now practicing in various locations throughout the United States. The institute philosophy is that ''Attachment is one of the most important concepts for us to understand, primarily because it affects our ability to form close relationships throughout our lives.''[3] Yet children who are adopted at older ages often have problems with attachment. Cline believes therapy is necessary ''to enable the unattached child to develop a strong, positive bond with his or her parents. . . .''[4]

Julie discovered that a therapist trained by Foster Cline

was practicing in a town about an hour's drive away. So once every week Julie and Steven made the two-hour round trip for this therapy. The therapist treated Steven for nine months. At that point there was little visible improvement, and the therapy was discontinued.

Nevertheless, by the time Steven reached junior high, life had improved for him. By ninth grade he was feeling good about himself. Playing defense on the school football team has brought him success. His grades are, in his words, "Fair—about C-plus."

What does he enjoy academically? "I like being in a mock trial and acting out a court session. I like the arguing in the trial. The other subjects I'm good in are history, religion and biology."

Steven says that he does not have any problems with race. "Most of my friends are white, but I have some black friends, too. I feel I fit in with people of both races. I feel fine with black people. It doesn't matter to me who I'm with. I'm not confused about my race. I'm black."

However, this was not always so, Steven remembers. "I did want to be white when I was in third grade. It didn't have anything to do with my parents, though. I went to an all-white school. Any black child would have had this problem. I got picked on a lot, but then I got over it. I grew bigger, and people didn't bug me a lot."

Steven says that having white parents was not a problem. But the frequent questions from strangers did bother him. "Explaining gets tiresome after the first five hundred times," he says. He excuses people who ask such questions. "It's confusing to people, seeing this family."

Steven seems to have less interest in his biological parents than does Mark. Steven says he has no feelings about being adopted or about his birth mother. Nevertheless, he is interested in his roots. "Tracing it way back, I'm partly South American Indian." But as to investigating his biological family, he says, "I have other things to think about right now."

Steven believes he has plenty of self-confidence, and he is looking forward to college. "I'm overconfident sometimes," he says. "I plan things too far ahead, and I'm very optimistic. I feel good about myself, but I would change my temper. When I get angry, it's not pretty."

TRANSRACIAL PARENTING

The first transracial adoptive families were pioneers. Their trial-and-error experiences can provide guidance for new generations of transracial adoptive families. In this chapter the adoptive father, Frank Lewis, views transracial adoption from the perspective of the African American adoptive parent in a biracial marriage. Two different approaches to the problem of racism are described, by Mark Soule and his mother Peggy Soule, and by John Raible. Therapist Jim Mahoney, who counsels adoptive families, offers advice for coping with racism in schools. Finally, we discuss the manual developed by the Michigan Department of Social Services for transracial foster and adoptive parents.

ATTACKING RACISM

From his experiences working with nonwhite adopted and foster children, therapist Jim Mahoney has developed a workshop on transracial parenting entitled ''Attacking Racism Before It Defeats Your Child.''[1] Adopted nonwhite children face a complex situation. They may act out their problems in school because they cannot talk about them.

In addition, they may face institutional racism at school, which may prevent them from succeeding.

"It is important," Mahoney tells parents in his workshop, "to prepare your children to resist bias and discrimination." Mahoney and the adoptive families develop a plan to help children of color succeed in a racist society. This plan includes helping the children succeed in school.

"How your kids are doing in school is how they will do later in life." Mahoney warns. "If a child of color does not graduate from high school, statistics show that his or her life span will be shorter than a white person's who has dropped out of high school."

To protect one's child, one has to confront institutional racism in school—such as the absence of African American staff, or the lack of library materials depicting African Americans. "Such activism can serve a dual purpose," he explains. "In addition to making changes in the school or the classroom, you will also show you personally oppose racism. You need to convey to children that you like their culture, cherish their color and looks, and above all that you will stand up to anyone who discriminates against them because of their color."

Become an activist, advise many experts. Children need to know you're against racism, that it's wrong.[2] Louise Derman-Sparks, the author of an antibias curriculum, advises parents to teach activism to young children. If the library or the school has few books about African Americans, write to the administration or start a campaign to purchase the books.

Hugh Scott, a dean of education and a former school superintendent in Washington, D.C., suggests the following steps:[3]

• Be a role model for your child. Demonstrate in your conduct and your talk that you oppose racist and discriminatory attitudes.

- Examine the textbooks of your school and check for negative stereotypes of minorities.

- Be willing to talk openly with your children about racism and discrimination, and be willing to listen to them.

- Insist on high goals.

THE IMPORTANCE OF THE COMMUNITY

Earlier, we introduced Frank Lewis, a black parent in a transracial family. The family consists of a white adoptive mother, Leslie; her two adopted sons, Gary and Brian; and Frank, whom Leslie married when the boys were eleven. Frank, an African American, was also a single adoptive parent. He too had an eleven-year-old son when he and Leslie married. Three years after their marriage, they adopted a three-year-old girl of Italian and African American heritage—the family's fourth child.

The problems were not as difficult as they had expected. "It kind of surprised us both that we had minimal problems," says Frank. "I think a big part of it is where we live. Before we married, we planned very carefully where we were going to live. After we were married, we moved into a very integrated community. A large number of interracial families are here and also a large number of adoptive families. It is a racially and culturally diverse community that is primarily middle class with some quite affluent sections. In the sixties it was the first town to voluntarily bus children in order to racially integrate the community schools."

Frank recommends that transracial families live in a well-integrated community. "The children need to associate with children of their own race for the sake of their self-image." Frank's feeling comes from his own youthful experiences in Pittsburgh, Pennsylvania. "I grew up in a fairly integrated community, but the parochial school I attended was practically all white. Out of a thousand students, there were maybe three black students in each grade. In looking back, I realize I had very few friends at school. I didn't think about it at the time, because I did have friends in the neighborhood where I lived. At times it felt awkward being such a small minority in the school. For example, in history class if there was a discussion about Africa, everyone would turn and look at me.

"Through that experience I gained the ability to understand and live with and work with just about everyone. So I always wanted to live in a diverse community. In an all-black community, I wouldn't be comfortable. I like the diversity. But I also learned from my own school situation, and I had decided I would not put my children in a situation where they would be such a small percentage of the total population."

The birth mother of Monique, the three-year-old whom Leslie and Frank Lewis adopted, had requested that the agency find an interracial Catholic couple, since she was a white Italian Catholic and the birth father was African American. "Monique had lived for two and one half years with her biological mother before being surrendered for adoption," Frank Lewis explains. "For the first month or two after Monique came to live with us, she would wake up in the middle of the night screaming. Fortunately therapy definitely helped her."

Recently, an incident of racial violence disrupted the life of the integrated town where the Lewis family lives and caused many painful feelings. "Monique felt threatened by these race divisions in the community," says Frank. "She felt torn apart. When people talked about not liking white people, she felt as if they were talking about her. When they said they didn't like black people, she also felt they were talking about her."

This is the sort of problem that can trouble mixed-race children brought up in a transracial family. Monique identifies with white people as well as with black people. "I think socially she considers herself black," says her father.

"We have stressed that when she is out in the world, people will initially view her as black. Emotionally and intellectually she knows she's interracial. I believe her racial self-image is a positive one."

Along with a positive racial image, the adopted child in a transracial family needs self-esteem. "Monique's self-esteem has to do with questions of adoption. Just recently she told Leslie about a dream she had. She dreamed she was in a room, up for adoption, and people were looking her over. The social worker came and put a 'sold' sign on her. It made her feel very sad. Leslie explained the process of adoption. Yes, money was exchanged, but it was for expenses and services, not for the sale of the child.

"I believe her self-esteem is high. She has many talents to fall back on. She can say that she's a good person or that she's good in dance and in gymnastics. Leslie and I don't want her self-esteem tied up with images of beauty. People often tell her how good-looking she is. For the last three or four years whenever that happens, Leslie and I always say, 'Yes, and she's also a very good kid,' just to let her know it isn't beauty alone that makes up her value. I think she was beginning to wonder if people would still like her if she wasn't good-looking.

"It's important for parents to acknowledge a child's racial and cultural background," Frank notes, "and it's important for kids to learn about the parents' racial and cultural background." He wouldn't advise a transracial family to live in an all-black neighborhood. "Parents have to be true to their own identity while fostering the child's identity.

"Leslie is of Irish background, so on Saint Patrick's Day we have an Irish dinner. We also have Irish music and talk about Ireland. We've gone to African American dance performances, and during black history month we get involved in the kids' projects. We also share our memories and experiences of the civil rights movement. It seems so long ago to the children."

Some of the problems of children in interracial adoptions come from the questions people ask about their unusual families. Frank recalls such an incident with the two boys Leslie adopted before their marriage.

"Shortly after our marriage, Gary and Brian came to me and asked if they could say they were my birth children by a previous marriage, and that I had remarried Leslie. It seemed they needed a new way to explain their white mother to their schoolmates. It wasn't a rejecting thing; it just would make them more acceptable to society. They didn't want to have to go into the story every time a question came up. They told me that when they said they were adopted, people would ask other questions. This was a way of ending the questions. I replied that I couldn't do that. They would be fooling themselves. It was better to deal with the situation than to make up stories."

FAMILY ATTITUDES TOWARD RACISM

Mark Soule, twenty-one years of age, and John Raible, in his early twenties, are both black Americans who were adopted at birth by white families before the 1972 informal ban on transracial adoption. They led a workshop at the 1990 North American Council on Adoptable Children convention in Washington, D.C., entitled "Black Adoptees Speak."

"My brothers and sisters are very understanding when it comes to a problem of race. They would always stick up for me when they heard racial insults," says Mark Soule.

"I think what Mark said is really important," says John Raible. "My brother and sister were not taught to be antiracist. It was very, very painful for me to be in situations—my brother and I are one year apart and shared the same friends—where racial jokes came up and my brother did not say anything. He opted to be comfortable and didn't say anything. That sent a really clear message to me. I knew my brother loved me, but that was a strange way to show it. *Your* brother learned, or was taught, that if someone slandered you racially, he should fight your battles with you."

Mark Soule's family illustrates the way a transracial family should try to cope with racism. John Raible's experience, on the other hand, seems to be an example of what not to do.

"I grew up in a predominantly white area, but I was never exposed just to whites," Mark Soule explained. "I'm a black American, and that's what I'll always consider myself. That's the way it's always been within my family, with my friends, and at school. I went from a predominantly white elementary school to a predominantly black high school, and that transition was very natural because we had an extended family of people of color.

"I was told what to expect in terms of racism before it ever happened. I was prepared for things when they were happening and I knew who to talk to when I had a problem of race. I could talk to my parents. They could understand, but there wasn't much they could relate to. But I could always talk to other people who could relate.

"I have been exposed to my heritage and my culture since I was very young. I think that's important to know, for people who have adopted children of color or who plan to adopt children of color in the future."

Peggy Soule, Mark's mother, remembers attending the adoption conference in 1972 at which the president of the NABSW denounced transracial adoptions. "The black adoptive parents were supportive of the transracial families," she recalls. "The black parents wanted the white parents to succeed with their adopted black children, but some white families attending the conference were disturbed by this denunciation of cross-racial adoption. They wondered if they had done a disservice to their children. I had confidence that I was a good parent. But I also knew we needed to connect with black issues and with more black parents."

This help and support from black families made an important difference in Mark Soule's life. Peggy continues, "The issues for us are adoption and the problem of racism. Whether the children are biracial or not, society sees them as black, and therefore they will face racism. White parents had to learn about racism if they were going to help their children. You need to feel good about yourself as a parent, but you also need to understand institutional racism."

In upstate New York, where the Soule family lives, the Episcopal church conducted two-day workshops throughout the diocese on the subject of institutional racism in an effort to make people more aware of the problem. Peggy Soule has six adopted children, four of whom are white. Her children know, she says, that "I would go to war against a racist comment. I would never accept an insensitive comment at school or anywhere. People must begin to respect the norms and values of other cultures," she says. "We're not trying to blend the cultures, but to be happy with the differences and with the different cultures."

THE MICHIGAN MANUAL

Some years ago the Michigan Department of Social Services rejected a white couple's petition to adopt a nonwhite child. The couple sued the department, and in 1986 the court ruled that an agency could not turn down a couple's request to adopt a child solely because of race. The agency was then compelled to consider applications for transracial adoption. Consequently it published guidelines for counselors to use in evaluating a transracial placement.

The Michigan Manual's purpose is "to assess the family's ability to value, respect, appreciate, and educate the child regarding the child's racial, ethnic, and cultural heritage and background." Is the family able to meet the needs of a child of another race?[4]

The manual notes that when children are forming a sense of self that includes their race, they need to know people of the same race. Racial identity needs include having black friends and schoolmates and knowing black adults who can serve as role models. To meet these needs, the manual suggests families may move into an integrated community, send the children to integrated schools, or join a black church.

The manual recommends giving children a positive picture of their race by attending concerts by black artists, buying children's books about important blacks, teaching black history, and going to movies about black people.

According to the Michigan Manual, parents should know how racism works and how to minimize its effects. Prospective adoptive parents must explore their own consciousness of racism in the community, in their family, and even in themselves. The family must acknowledge that cross-racial adoption makes them an interracial family forever, and this will affect them all.

If the Raibles had had the benefit of this guide, they might have been better able to combat racism. Mark Soule was fortunate in that his family was sensitive to these points when they adopted him.

The interracial family will often attract attention. Black children who love and depend on their white parents will be questioned by adults and children, black and white, about their feelings about being in an interracial family. Children on the school playground may ask black adopted children what it is like to have white parents. The adopted children may not know how to say they are the only parents they have ever lived with, so they do not know about having other parents. Many of the children interviewed for this book remarked on the pain these questions caused them—especially "after the thousandth time" they were asked.

Families need to talk openly about racial situations that each family member experiences. Families can prepare their black children by anticipating situations and advising ways to handle them.

Prospective parents can ask themselves questions to

determine if they can empathize with the experience of their children. Have the parents ever felt like a minority someplace? Are they in touch with other white families that have adopted children? What knowledge do they have of black history and of the black community? Will they learn about black history and black achievements in dance, theater, music, and literature?

Answering these questions may help create successful transracial adoptions.

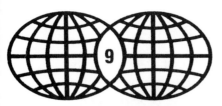

INTERNATIONAL ADOPTIONS: CHILDREN FROM KOREA

Wars make orphans. World War II, the Korean War, and the Vietnam War have all contributed to the increase in international adoptions. After World War II, adoptive homes were found in the United States for some orphans from Western Europe. Although of a different nationality and culture, these children were the same race as the white families that adopted them.

KOREAN WAR ORPHANS

During the Korean War (1950–1953) many Korean-American children were fathered by American soldiers with Korean women. These children of American fathers and Korean mothers had several strikes against them. As mixed-race children, they were often spurned by native Koreans, and because they were born outside marriage, they had no legal rights and no right to an education, according to Korean tradition.

In Korea, as in other Asian nations, family ties are very important. The respect for the family makes the extended family very strong; however, as a result of the emphasis on family, people are reluctant to adopt a child not connected to them by a family tie. Thus, orphans and abandoned children have little hope of being adopted by other Koreans.

In Korea the mixed-race children were called ''dust of the streets.'' Knowing the disadvantages their children would face, some of the Korean birth mothers allowed their children to be adopted by American families. Unlike the World War II orphans of Western Europe, these children differed from their adoptive parents not only in nationality and culture, but also in race.

Transracial foreign adoptions began with a small number of American adoptions from Korea in the 1950s. Since then hundreds of thousands of white families in the United States have adopted children from foreign countries, and most of them have been interracial adoptions. Although in the 1970s and 1980s many children were adopted from South and Central America and southern Asia, more children were adopted from Korea than from any other country. In the 1990s the South Korean government has begun to limit the number of children from orphanages who could be adopted by non-Koreans and leave Korea. Unfortunately the number of children being adopted within Korea is not increasing, and as a result Korean orphanages are now severely overcrowded.

INTERNATIONAL ADOPTIONS TODAY

''Why were 8,327 foreign-born nonwhite children adopted by white American families in 1984 when anywhere from 50,000 to 100,000 children in United States foster care were legally free for adoption?'' asks Howard Altstein, the adoption researcher.[1] Altstein points out that ''in 1983 approximately two million U.S. families attempted to adopt parentless children. Less than 3 percent were able to do so.''[2] The number of children in the United States who are legally free for adoption has decreased. Altstein notes that the Los Angeles County Adoption Agency, one of the largest adoption agencies in the United States, placed ten times fewer children in adoptive homes in 1975 than it had placed in 1965, before the 1972 objection to transracial adoptions. Yet, he says, the desire for healthy adoptable infants has increased since the 1960s.

The children available for adoption in the United States are older and many are nonwhite. According to Altstein, "Many agencies continue to frown upon and discourage adoption across racial lines. . . . In contrast, the procedures involved for an intercountry adoption are comparatively simple and the results in many cases are remarkably quick." Hence the number of intercountry adoptions.[3]

CHERYLL AND EILEEN FROM KOREA

The first families that adopted from Korea in the late 1950s and the early 1960s were probably unaware of the need for sensitivity to the race and culture of the adopted child. As with domestic adoptions, time and experience brought parents and social workers to recognize this need.

International Adoptions Inc., an agency (now called Wide Horizons for Children), placed many Korean children in American homes. Phyllis Lowenstein, former director of the agency, discussed these adoptions with two young Korean women who were adopted as children—Cheryll Perry and Eileen Thompson. Cheryll Perry was six years old when she was adopted from a Korean orphanage in the early 1960s and brought to the United States. "My adopted uncle was in Korea at that time," says Cheryll, "and he wrote to my mother about the children there. My parents already had two biological sons, but my mother wanted a daughter."[4]

So the Perrys adopted Cheryll—the first Korean child in the town where she grew up in Maine. "It was very hard growing up," she recalls. "Everyone in the community stared at me because I was different. I never met other adoptive children like me. That's why it was hard, too. It's so great today—the process of adoption—because families have support and help now, which my mother didn't have."

"This is very important," confirms Phyllis Loewenstein. "Parents are hooked up with other families who have adopted internationally so their children will not experience the kind of isolation that Cheryll did. These adopted children get to know lots of other families where the kids don't match the parents. They're not the only ones."[5]

"High school and adolescence were very, very hard," says Cheryll. "Dating was hard in high school. Boys in my high school liked me mostly as a friend."

The issue of looking different from her parents was difficult, also. "It's the first thing you realize when you look in the mirror," Cheryll says, "that you look different from your mother and father. You can't deny that. I felt I was Caucasian inside, like my mother and father, but when I looked in the mirror I realized that I had Asian features and that there was nothing I could do about it."

Cheryll describes her parents' attitudes: "My parents were more attuned to assimilation, making me feel like I was the same as the others in the family." This is a well-intentioned and loving approach, but denying an obvious racial difference does not work. "Love is not enough," says Loewenstein. "You must help children learn about differences. It's ridiculous to deny differences, because they are real. A child must be able to be proud of differences. But parents can also emphasize those things about the children that are the same as the parents. For example, you can say to the child that she has the same laugh as her mother, or to the boy that he's as tall as his uncle."

Eileen Thompson is another Korean woman who was adopted as a child and brought to Massachusetts when she was about two years old. "It's important for the child to acknowledge the difference and then move on," she says. "The parent must help the child accept all parts of himself.

Our parents did not have the help and support with this that parents have now."[6]

"You must be proud of your Asian heritage," says Cheryll. "It was hard being in a town where everyone was Caucasian except me. I wanted to be blond and blue-eyed. When people stared at me, I never thought I was attractive. Strangers will look at you a little oddly when you're with your family. They're thinking, how did that happen?"

BEN ADAMS

Ben, a fifteen-year-old high school student, was born in Korea and was eight months old when he was adopted and brought to this country. His adoptive parents already had two biological daughters, one six years old, the other four.

His adoptive mother says that Ben was a happy baby. "Ben had been well taken care of in a foster home in Korea. As a baby he smiled whenever someone called his name," she recalls. From second to fifth grade, Ben went to a Montessori school, and in sixth grade he was enrolled in the public school in the suburban town where they live.

"Ben is bright," says his mother, Ann Adams, "but the sixth grade was the beginning of a disorganization for him." His mother, a teacher with a master's degree in special education, is aware of the importance of school in the child's life. She is also sensitive to the harmful effects that racism in school can have on a young student.

"The school was a monster; there were three separate buildings. In seventh grade there was a lot of name calling. There were a lot of things that hurt him, but he never told me too much about them. There were a couple of other Asian kids in the school, but Ben never saw them. Some students called him a gook. And he was called Chinese. He was on the school lacrosse team, and at the end of one game, when the teams lined up to shake hands, a player on the opposite team made a racist comment. Later the coach made the boy apologize to Ben, and Ben was embarrassed even more by the apology. I told him that I understood those things made him angry. And there were, of course, hitting incidents too. I told him, just don't bloody anybody.

"As to the adoption, when he was in fourth grade a friend asked him a lot of questions about his birth mother. Where was she? I overheard them discussing the adoption. Ben handled it well. He didn't keep it a secret.

"He's never said to me, 'I want to find my birth mother.' I never felt threatened by that. I would like to go back to Korea and share that trip with him. I have a friend who adopted a Korean child and was scared that one day the boy would go back to Korea and find his birth mother."

Ben says, "I have two mothers, but my birth mother has no significance for me. I don't consider her my mother; she is a total stranger now. I have no feelings about her. I do wonder why my birth mother put me up for adoption, though. Did she have too many children, or was she a prostitute? It wouldn't bother me too much either way, but I'd like to know. If she was a prostitute I'd have no respect for her, but if she couldn't take care of me, then I would respect that.

"Sometimes I feel a little awkward when friends first see me with my family. But, hey, they have to accept that I'm adopted. And I do get all these questions; it gets to be annoying. I never wanted to look like my parents; I'm happy to be who I am. Sometimes I'm around my parents and I'll forget that I'm Oriental. Then I look in the mirror and reality hits again. It doesn't matter much to me.

"Under the Korean Exchange Student Program, a lot of seniors from Korea came to our high school to finish school. They were cool. I'd talk to them. I would like to go back to Korea and see my birthplace, and I would like to learn more about Korean culture, but I wouldn't want to live there. I wouldn't survive in Korea; their schools are so hard, and Korean education is very strict. My teacher says I have potential, but I don't apply myself. I guess that's true, but I don't have the dedication. I'd like to meet other Koreans. There's one thing we have in common—our background. But it wouldn't make our friendship stronger. It's who we are, not where we're from, that's important.

"There's lots of racism, of course. The kids used to call me Chinese Eyes. The racist remarks never cut me deeply. My mother conditioned me for that. When I was about four, I talked with my mother about kids calling me names in school. We drove around in the car and we talked about it. She said that people who did that had problems themselves. It didn't happen that often. As I got older it sort of stopped."

Ben's mother says that the family learned about Korean culture. "We tried Korean cooking, and I bought beautiful ceremonial Korean dresses for my daughters. I found a book for adopted children called *Filling in the Blanks*. We read it together for a while. Ben enjoys taking out his baby book and going through it. His passport is there and his Korean name.

"When Ben was four, an eighteen-year-old Vietnamese foster son came to live with us for four and a half years. Ben was eight when Hung left. He was a good role model for Ben. Hung now works as a draftsman for an airplane company and also does landscaping. He has married a Japanese woman.

"Ben is a great kid. He has some problems with self-esteem though. He is bright, but he has some problems in school. He likes to draw. He puts down his artwork, but he knows how much I enjoy his work. He likes architecture, and he has the fine motor skills for that kind of work. He could construct wonderful things with Lego blocks when he was three."

Of Ben's other interests, his mother says, "I sent some of Ben's poems and stories that he wrote in school to a young authors magazine, and one of them was published. My husband coaches lacrosse teams, and Ben plays lacrosse and likes wrestling."

Ben says, "I'm critical of my art, I see everything that's wrong. But I like to draw buildings, and I could be an architect's assistant. I would like to be an architect, but I don't have the math.

"I'm close to both of my sisters. They are so liberal. My dad is really straight. He likes everything to be the way it's supposed to be. He says, 'This is what they do in this society.' But he lets me do a lot of things. This summer he's letting me go white-water rafting with my friends. I like the outdoors. I like rock climbing and hiking."

INTERNATIONAL ADOPTIONS: CHILDREN FROM LATIN AMERICA

DAMIEN AND PETER

Damien, who is thirteen, left an orphanage in São Paulo, Brazil, to come to the United States when he was eight years old. He had been brought to the orphanage soon after he was born. When he was several months old he went to live with an adoptive family who had five daughters and apparently wanted a son. But when Damien was eight years old, the family returned him to the orphanage.

How did Damien feel about this? "I was feeling sad because they were throwing me out," he says. He did not like the orphanage in São Paulo. "It was poor," he says. "There weren't many things, like sheets, blankets. And the boys bothered you. There were fights and they stole from you. There were seventeen kids in one house. It was boring, too. We just sat around all day; we didn't go to school."

The orphanage, according to Damien's American father, Carey, who visited it, is one of the best in the country. But an orphanage is still an orphanage. Damien's father says that the children were well cared for, although it was poor. A housemother and housefather lived with the boys and watched over them.

Carey had chosen to apply for a foreign adoption because he had almost no chance of adopting an American child. He registered with an American agency, and its Brazilian representative sent him the files and pictures of several boys who were free for adoption. "Damien immediately stood out when I saw his picture. I don't know. There was something about him," explains his father.

"After I was at the orphanage for about six months, the people explained to me that a person would adopt me. They gave me an album with pictures of my dad," Damien recalls. Then "the orphanage people took me to the court, and the judge asked me if I wanted to go to the United States. I told the judge, yes. I didn't want to stay at the orphanage, and I wanted to have a family." A couple of weeks later my dad came and picked me up at the orphanage. That was the first time we met. We got along pretty well right away."

In 1986 Damien's white father adopted him through an agency, LIMIAR, that operates several orphanages in Brazil. Carey traveled to Brazil to complete the adoption. After a week in São Paulo, Damien and his new father went to Rio de Janeiro for a week to arrange for immigration visas through the American consulate. Then they flew to the United States.

"I wanted to get away from Brazil because I had a bad life there," says Damien. "When I came to New York City, it was exciting because everything was so different. I liked that. I didn't know English then. I still spoke my language, Portuguese. My dad didn't know any Portuguese. He had a translation list in Portuguese and English. He would read the translation from the list when he wanted to tell me something. We came to New York in the summer. I went to classes in English on Saturdays.

"When I started school, I had problems. The kids in the school were white, Chinese, and Spanish. They teased me that I was adopted. My dad told me to ignore them. He told me I was special. After a while they just stopped.

"Kids found out I was adopted because my dad explained to them when some came to my house. You know, he looks different from me. Then when they got mad at me, they passed it on to other kids, so all the kids knew I was adopted.

"Once my best friend, who is Spanish, asked me why my dad and I look different. I explained it to him. Sometimes I don't explain it to people. It depends. My best friend has a stepfather. That's not so different from me."

Damien lives in a mixed but largely Latin American neighborhood. He says, "I think I fit in with both Latinos and North Americans. When I first came here, it was hard to get used to, because the kids were nothing like me. Now I don't feel that way anymore."

Damien never saw his mother because she left him at birth. Is he curious about her? "Sometimes I wonder what she was like," admits Damien. "Sometimes I feel sad."

Two years after adopting Damien, Carey adopted a second son, Peter, also from Brazil, because he believed it would be good for Damien to have a brother like him. Peter had also had a painful childhood; when he was five years old his mother died, and then his sister died.

"When Peter first came, I was jealous," says Damien. "Before he came, I got a lot of attention and I could do what I wanted. Then the attention went to him, and I had to stay home and baby-sit him. But now I do think of him as my brother, and I'm happy that he's here."

CECILIA AND HER ADOPTED BROTHER, RAFAEL

Cecilia was eight and a half in 1984 when she and her mother, Alice James, traveled to Brazil to bring home her adopted infant brother, a successful and happy event. "I remember having to sleep on the plane because it was such a long trip to Brazil. Then we switched planes, and when we arrived it was dark. I remember being excited and wondering what he looked like," Cecilia recalls.

"When we first saw him he was sleeping and I remember thinking he looked so ugly, and I thought, Oh, no, we have an ugly one. Then when I saw him awake I thought, he's so cute. We all lived in a little house while we waited for the adoption papers to go through. I remember being in that small town in Brazil and the poverty. Little kids came begging at our door, and we gave away a lot of my clothes.

"For a long time my mother had been thinking about adopting, and I thought it would be nice. I was kind of surprised that it was a boy, because I had thought it would be a girl and I would have a little sister. I don't have any other brothers or sisters, so I remember wondering what it would be like to have a brother."

The small orphanage had arranged for Rafael's biological mother to meet Alice and Cecilia. Rafael's biological mother had two children by her first husband, who had deserted her and the children. Rafael's father also abandoned her after she became pregnant. She was sick, and it was impossible for her to raise a third child alone. When Rafael was born, she took him to the orphanage, where he stayed for three months.

"I remember meeting his mother," Cecilia says, "and I felt sad that she had to give him up because she couldn't take care of him. She came and visited with us for a little while. She was really beautiful; she had long black hair. She held Rafael kind of awkwardly for a picture that my mother took. I remember thinking, Now my mother is his mother because she is taking care of him." His birth mother told the social worker after the visit that she was happy that Rafael was with Alice and Cecilia.

"We returned to Rio next and stayed in a hotel," Cecilia continues. "I remember going on trips around Rio with him in a little basket and going to the beach and to get his picture taken for the passport. Then we went home with him on the plane. He looked so little, lying in the bassinet at our feet on the plane.

"Having an adopted brother is just like having any other brother, as far as I can tell. He's annoying and spoiled, but he's very cute, too. He has a lot of different traits that are usually not found in our family, which is kind of interesting. He's different from me. I like to write poetry and read a lot. He likes to draw, and he's good at music, and he likes sports. I guess that happens in other families, too."

Cecilia says that people always ask her if she's baby-sitting when they see her with her brother because he is a different color than she is. When she tells them that he is her brother, they are surprised. "I have to go into the whole story that he's from Brazil and he's adopted. People think it's really great, though, when you tell them about the adoption."

A TYPICAL FOREIGN ADOPTION

In general, adopting a child from a foreign country is simpler and faster than adopting an American child, which is almost always fraught with difficulty and delay. Many adoptive parents have decided to adopt internationally because it seemed simpler; adopting in the United States took a long time and was filled with uncertainty. However, international adoptions can be unpredictable as well, and people often have bad experiences. In 1981 thirteen parents who had adopted children in Brazil were stopped at the airport in Rio de Janeiro and were prevented from leaving the country with their children.

The procedures Alice followed are fairly typical of a foreign adoption arranged through an American agency. First she attended an informational meeting at which the agency representative covered certain topics:

- the requirements for adopting in other countries

- the countries in which the agency has orphanages or child-care centers

- the possible age of the children

- the length of time one could expect to wait

- the costs

- the agency procedures

The costs vary, depending on the country. For example, children were escorted from Korea to the United States by a social worker, so a percentage of the worker's air fare was paid by the adoptive parents. For Brazilian adoptions, the adoptive parents traveled to Brazil to fetch the child and paid for their own transportation. Fees included the cost for the adoption home study and the social workers' interviews. There are court costs in the United States, as well as court costs and child-care costs in the country where the child was born.

After the informational meeting, Alice met with the social worker at an individual interview to discuss her reasons for adopting, her ability to care for a second child, and the country she should adopt from. In her case, it was Brazil. Important issues discussed also included her ability to parent a nonwhite child and to respect the culture of the child's native country.

The home study followed. This evaluation of the home by a licensed social worker is required by law before any type of legal adoption can take place. This agency also required that all adoptive parents attend a weekend of intensive workshops on international adoption.

Once these steps were completed, the papers, including the home study report and the birth certificate, were sent to the agency in Brazil. At this point the waiting began. Waiting is a major part of the adoption process. Alice had first asked for a girl, since she thought Cecilia and the child would be close as sisters. However, several other prospective parents had designated girls, and they were ahead on the lists. After several months, the counselor called to say that there was a little boy two weeks old at the orphanage and no one to adopt him. Alice decided to take the child.

At this point Cecilia recalls an endless round of visits to family court, the immigration office, and the passport office, and reams of forms to be filled out and notarized. When the baby's birth certificate and release for adoption arrived from Brazil, they were submitted to the Department of Immigration. A special visa for dependents was needed to bring the adopted child into the country. In addition, there were legal papers to be filed in the family court in her district regarding the adoption in Brazil. Finally all the paperwork was done, the passports were in order, the visa had come through. With all their papers in hand, Alice James and Cecilia left for Brazil. After Rafael's formal adoption, the three returned to the United States.

INTERNATIONAL TEENAGERS

A number of teenagers who were adopted from foreign countries as children have spoken about their experiences. A panel of these young people talked about the problems of racism and cultural differences at the convention of the North American Council on Adoptable Children in 1990. Because of the earlier experiences of children such as Eileen and Cheryll, adoptive parents have been sensitive and alert to the problems that can be caused by ignoring cultural and racial differences.

Tim, sixteen years old, is from Vietnam. His sister Meredith, thirteen years old, is white and is a birth child. There are four children in all in the family, which resides in a well-to-do California suburb.

''There are a handful of Asians in my school and a lot of white kids,'' says Tim. ''I feel I have to prove myself because I'm different. The hardest times are the transitions from one school to another. The other Asian kids are pushed to achieve by their parents. My parents want me to be well rounded and not just concentrate on the academic side. The Asians get picked on, but not as much as the black kids. Like on the football team, there are only a few black kids. The other kids say to them, the only reason the coach picked you is because you're black and he's black—stuff like that.''

Tim has experienced racism, however. He was called Charlie by other boys. His parents explained that that was the name for the Vietcong soldiers during the Vietnam War. Along with the racist slur, it bothered him that it was the name for the enemy.

His thirteen-year-old sister says, ''I get a lot of questions when Tim picks me up after school. Kids ask, 'Who's that guy?' I don't resent it, though. I sort of like the attention. While I'm around, most conversations are not racist,'' Meredith admits. ''The kids seem to have more respect for other races when I'm around.''

Donna, who is fifteen years old and in the tenth grade, was born in Colombia and adopted as a baby. She has an adopted sister, eighteen, who was also born in Colombia. Donna says of the problem of racism, ''If it gets out of hand I ask my mom to intervene. I can only take so much of it.''

Donna echoes the memories of other children growing up. ''I asked my mom when I was three years old, 'Why am I not white like you are? Is my skin just dirty or something?' My mother said, 'It's just the way God made you.' ''

Fourteen-year-old Anita, who is in the ninth grade, is from Bangladesh. She lives with her white adoptive parents and two adopted brothers who are black. ''There is a lot of prejudice in my school,'' she says. ''It's mostly white. They know my brothers are black, and they criticize them. They tell me I'm acting black.''

THE SEARCH FOR BIRTH PARENTS

The teenagers differ in their attitudes toward their birth parents—a central issue in all adoptions. Scott, a seventeen-year-old from Korea, does not want to search for his birth parents. He feels it would be "disloyal and ungrateful for what my parents have done for me."

But thirteen-year-old Amy, also from Korea and in the eighth grade, says that she would like to go back and find her birth parents.

Kimberly, an adopted Korean girl of fifteen, is one of five children. She says, "I want to know who my birth parents were. I think I have the right to know."

And Dana, also fifteen years old, from Colombia, says, "If I had the option to meet my birth parents, my mother or father, I would choose it, but I wouldn't go back to look for them. What questions would I have? I would ask, 'Why did you give me up?' I know Colombia is a poor country, but still . . ." In school, when Dana is asked to draw a family tree, she writes in her adopted parents. "I don't see any reason to bring up my biological parents in school. My adopted parents are my real parents. I'm extremely close to them."

Jamie, who is from Korea, mentions her fear of what might happen at a meeting with her birth parents. "Bad feelings might come back if I asked them, 'Why did you give me up?' "

Anita says that someone did go to Bangladesh to search for her parents, but unsuccessfully. "I would go over and try to find my brothers and sisters," she concludes.

The teens also differ in their interest in the culture of the countries where they were born. Scott feels he has to go to too many Korean cultural and ethnic events. He wants more time for his regular school and sports activities. "I'm busy," he complains.

Kimberly did have a chance to visit Korea. She says, "I went back a few years ago with a teen group, so I don't really want to go now. But I wasn't a minority there, and that was different." And Tim says he "has fun with the culture things. I don't mind going to them." Most of the teens thought that cultural awareness contributed to their positive self-image.

A SCIENTIFIC STUDY

A study of intercountry adopted children was conducted in 1990 by Howard Altstein and Rita James Simon, the sociologists who conducted the twenty-year study described in Chapter 4.[1] The research was begun in 1987 with the intention of measuring the psychosocial development of cross-culturally adopted children. There was some thought that the cultural difference added to the race difference might complicate the adjustment of these children.

Two groups of adoptive parents cooperated with the researchers. They interviewed 80 adoptive parents, 68 adopted children, and 28 birth children. About 50 percent of the children came from Korea, 25 percent from Latin America, and another 25 percent from Asian countries such as India.

The adoptive parents were highly educated, many having done postgraduate work, and had middle to high incomes. About 65 percent lived in all or mostly white neighborhoods. Of the 80 families, 57 had adopted children who were then under one year of age. Three-fourths of the parents had studied the culture of their adopted children.

The critical factor in the success of these adoptions was the age of the children at the time of the adoption. This result is found in all adoption research, regardless of race or culture. Many children who were more than two years old at the time of the adoption had missed the bonding experience and had had traumatic experiences in their native culture. For example, one Salvadorean boy had seen his parents shot before his eyes. Other children had been on the streets for several years before being picked up and adopted. Some had been sexually or physically abused.

Howard Altstein has been interviewed on his study. He has been asked if there are higher numbers of adoptees in alcohol treatment programs and in the courts and in detention programs.

"There are no higher rates of delinquency or mental illness or suicide in our study," he responds. "But adoptive parents are much more likely to seek professional help. Are adoptees more disturbed children? That's not clear. What is passed over in a birth child is not passed over in the adopted child. Are adopted children overrepresented in therapy and inpatient treatment residences? Yes. Are they therefore more in need of treatment? I think [they are there] not because of a greater disturbance but because of greater parental awareness."[2]

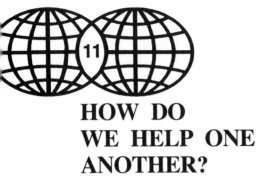

HOW DO
WE HELP ONE
ANOTHER?

PARENT GROUPS

Much of our information about transracial adoption has come from the parents and children themselves. The researchers who investigated the rate of success and the special problems in transracial adoptions could not have done so without the cooperation of the parent groups that the adoptive families formed. These groups are, in many ways, the most important organizations in the area of transracial adoption.

The American families who adopted children from Korea following the Korean War were the pioneers in transracial adoption in America. The Korean children, the first to be adopted transracially in significant numbers, ranged in age from toddlers to adolescents. These children had been scarred by war and had lost their families; they had also been transported to a foreign country to live with adoptive families whose culture, language, and race were different from their own.

When the children arrived, the American families were ill-equipped to handle many of the types of behavior, food preferences, language barriers, religious differences, and attitudes about the roles of men and women that their adopted children brought with them. There were no programs to prepare the adoptive parents for the differences between Korean and American society or to instruct them in Korean culture.

Out of a need to learn how to solve such problems the first parents groups were formed. As the adoptive parents met and shared experiences, they discovered that many of them were having similar difficulties. One mother described how she had learned to cook some Korean dishes for her ten-year-old adopted son. Serving him familiar food eased his adjustment to a foreign land. Several other parents benefited from her experience and found that this helped their children who were homesick for Korea. Other parents told of their success and failures in coping with their adopted child's adjustment difficulties. Out of these first meetings a network of parent support groups developed. Parents helped one another, discussed problems together, and exchanged solutions that were unknown at the time to professionals. As more was learned, and the parents saw that some of their children's needs were not being met through parent groups alone, the groups became involved in political action.

The Open Door Society was one of the first of the national coalitions of local parent groups. Families who were members exchanged information about Korean customs and history to share with their children. The society became a model for other parent support groups.

In the 1960s, when transracial adoption became more common, groups of parents organized so their children would know other families in which the parents were white and the children were black. The parents sought information about subjects as diverse as hair and skin care for their black children; how to handle racial prejudice; and the role of African Americans in history, the arts, and science. They also sought adult role models for their children. The children came to know one another socially and enjoyed the camaraderie of being with others who looked like them and lived in racially mixed families.

The Latin American Parents Association (LAPA) grew in response to the many families adopting children from Central and South America.

Typical parent groups are self-help organizations ranging in size from a small number of people who meet locally to large national organizations that provide adoption advice, sponsor conferences, and make donations of goods and money to orphanages. Single adoptive parent groups are active in most cities. Korean and Latin American culture camps meet for a week or two each summer, and adoptive family camping weekends take place across the country each year. Specialized travel agencies have developed that aid families going overseas to adopt a child. They also arrange homeland tours for adoptive parents and older adoptees.

The North American Council on Adoptable Children, the largest of the parent groups, is a national organization that developed when local chapters of the Council on Adoptable Children joined together to lobby, research, educate, and promote mental health and family stability for adoptive families.

The NACAC states its overall mission: "Every child has the right to a permanent family. The Council advocates the right of every child to a permanent, continuous, nurturing, and culturally sensitive family, and presses for the legal adoptive placement of any child denied that right."[1]

This organization has been involved with transracial adoption for many years. In 1981 it stated that "placement of children with a family of like ethnic background is desirable because such families are likely to provide the children with skills and strengths that counter the ill effects of racism." However, in special situations, such as sibling groups of mixed ethnic background, it argues for flexibility. "While supporting same race placements . . . some children may need to be placed transracially rather than continue to wait in foster care."[2]

In 1988 the NACAC suggested ten steps that government officials should take to advance minority adoptions, and it committed itself to full support for minority adoptive parent groups. In 1990 the NACAC urged that programs be developed to encourage placement of all children with foster and adoptive families of the same race. It has begun a federally funded survey of adoption agencies' practices in encouraging minority adoptive families. It is also trying to identify procedures that cause minority families to drop out of the adoption process.

A 1990 survey of same-race and transracial adoption practice conducted by the NACAC noted that "no discussion of same-race or transracial adoption in America would be complete without some mention of the distinction existing between policies appropriate for infants of color and those promulgated for older or handicapped minority children. One common thread seemed to link the responses and replies of almost all interviewees: while insistence upon same-race placement may be entirely plausible for healthy infants [children under two], it becomes much more problematic when older and other harder-to-place children are involved. Many agencies stated that same-race placement is good with infants, but it begins to fall apart in older and foster adoptions."[3]

EPILOGUE

BECAUSE EVERY CHILD NEEDS A FAMILY

The logo of the Black Adoption Services of Three Rivers Adoption Council in Pittsburgh, Pennsylvania, contains the following words: *because every child needs a family*. The North American Council on Adoptable Children states its mission in the words: *Every child has the right to a permanent family*. All advocacy groups for children agree on this need for a family. It is understood that this means a family capable of nurturing the unique individual that is the child.

Yet we are faced with a seeming paradox. In 1990, more than 36,000 children were awaiting permanent adoptive homes. In the same period, many people who wanted to adopt a child were discouraged by the extreme difficulty they encountered when trying to adopt. Legislative investigations have documented the existence of obstacles to adoption within the child welfare systems. These obstacles keep children waiting for nurturing homes.

Advocates for children plead that more be done to give homes to these waiting children. They do not suggest that adoption be made easy; there should be the most rigorous screening of families before adoption takes place. But many experts do decry the bureaucratic and legal tangles that obstruct good adoptions.

At times, the attitudes of adoption workers and agencies toward transracial adoption create an obstacle—one that may amount to a ban on such adoptions. Professionals who have both a right and a duty to screen prospective families carefully must realize that while race is an important consideration, it is not the only one.

Parents and children in transracial adoptive families do not deny that the race difference in their families is significant. However, they believe that the crucial fact that the adopted child must come to terms with is the loss of the original family. The child's deepest wound is this first loss, and the child often perceives it as abandonment by the original parent. Fears of abandonment haunt these children. For this wound to heal, the child must find a second family, and as quickly as possible.

The question before the adoption and foster care agencies is how long should a child be kept waiting for a family. Most people agree that an agency should aggressively seek African American parents for African American children. Agencies should modify their procedures in order to help make adoption more possible for African American parents, including making financial subsidies available. But if no black parent is found, and there is a white parent available to adopt a four- or five-year-old black child, what should the agency do? If this child is kept waiting for black parents until he or she is seven or nine years old, the child will most likely be too old, or too troubled, for any family—black or white—to be able to adopt.

A loving family is most important in the growth and development of children. To prolong the wait of the more than 36,000 children awaiting parents is to prolong the sense of abandonment that each one feels. With the increased efforts to encourage agencies to facilitate minority adoptions, and to assist minority families to adopt, and with the reevaluation of transracial adoption, perhaps the wait of some of these children can be ended.

SOURCE NOTES

CHAPTER 2

1. North American Council on Adoptable Children, *The Adoption Assistance and Child Welfare Act of 1980: The First Ten Years* (St. Paul, Minn.: NACAC, 1990).
2. Ibid.
3. Sonia Nazario, "Identity Crisis: When White Parents Adopt Black Babies, Race Often Divides," *Wall Street Journal*, Sept. 12, 1990, p. 1.
4. Ibid.
5. NACAC.
6. Ibid.
7. North American Council on Adoptable Children and the Transracial Debate (pamphlet published by North American Council, 1991), St. Paul, Minn., p. 37.
8. Ibid.
9. Ibid., p. 38.

CHAPTER 4

1. Quoted by Walter Leavy in "Should Whites Adopt Black Children?" *Ebony*, Sept. 1987, p. 76.

2. Ibid.
3. Ibid., p. 78.
4. Rita J. Simon and Howard Altstein, *Transracial Adoptees and Their Families: A Study of Identity and Commitment* (New York: Praeger, 1987), p. 9.
5. Leavy, p. 82.
6. Ruth G. McRoy and Louis A. Zurcher, *Transracial and Inracial Adoptees: The Adolescent Years* (Springfield, Ill.: Charles C Thomas, 1983).
7. Workshop, Fifteenth North American Training Conference on Adoptable Children: Celebrate Children, Focus on Adoption, Arlington, Va., August 16–19, 1990.
8. Simon and Altstein, p. 141.
9. Ibid., p. 142.

CHAPTER 5

1. J. C. Barden, "Washington Cedes Control of Its Foster Care Programs," *New York Times*, July 15, 1991. p. B1.
2. Barbara Sabol, New York State Legislature Joint Public Hearing on New York State Public Adoption System. Chairs: Senator Mary Goodhue and Assemblyman Albert Vann, May 3, 1990.
3. Ibid.
4. Walter Mondale et al., *The Adoption Assistance and Child Welfare Act of 1980: The First Ten Years* (St. Paul, Minn.: North American Council on Adoptable Children, 1990), p. 1.
5. NACAC, *Parent Group Manual* (St. Paul, Minn.: North American Council on Adoptable Children, 1990).
6. Ibid.
7. Sabol.
8. Senator Mary Goodhue, New York State Legislature Joint Public Hearing.
9. Sabol.

CHAPTER 7

1. Workshop, "Parenting Transracially," NACAC Training Conference, Arlington, Va., August 16–19, 1990.
2. Ibid.
3. "Attachment: Crisis in Older Adoption" (Evergreen, Colo.: Attachment Center, Evergreen Institute, 1990).
4. Ibid.

CHAPTER 8

1. NACAC Training Conference, Aug. 16–19, 1990.
2. Quoted by Mahoney, ibid.
3. Quoted by Mahoney, ibid.
4. "Cross-racial, Cross-parenting Assessment Guide," State of Michigan Department of Social Services, Manual Bulletin, Aug. 20, 1986 (Lansing, Mich.: Division of Children and Youth), pp. 2–13.

CHAPTER 9

1. Simon and Altstein, p. 132.
2. Ibid., p. 132.
3. Ibid., p. 133.
4. Videotape, Asian Focus Television, WGBH, Boston, Mass., 1986.
5. Ibid.
6. Ibid.

CHAPTER 10

1. A Study of Intercountry Adopted Children Workshop, NACAC training conference: Celebrate Children, Focus on Adoption, Arlington, Va., August 16–19, 1990.
2. Ibid.

CHAPTER 11

1. NACAC and the Transracial Adoption Debate (North American Council on Adoptable Children, St. Paul, Minn., 1991), p. 39.
2. Ibid., p. 37.
3. Ibid., pp. 37–38.

GLOSSARY

Adoptee: Any person whose birth parent relinquishes all legal right to care and custody so that the child can legally become the child of adoptive parents.

Adoption: A legal proceeding in which a court declares a person who is not a child's biological parent to be the child's legal parent, making the relationship permanent.

Adoptive parent: An adult who, through the legal process of adoption, becomes the legal and custodial parent of a child born to another.

Association of Black Social Workers (ABSW): A national organization of black social workers that is well known for its public stance against transracial adoption.

Birth parent: The biological parent.

Child welfare system: A multitude of agencies and services created to provide care for children living in their own families, in substitute families, or in institutions.

Child Welfare League of America (CWLA): The largest privately supported nonprofit organization in North

America devoted to helping deprived, neglected, and abused children and their families. CWLA formulates public policy on children's welfare and sets high standards for social work practice. According to CWLA the important issues in child welfare today are adolescent pregnancy, day care, child abuse and neglect, out-of-home care, adoption, and family support.

Civil rights movement: The effort to obtain equal rights for African Americans, as guaranteed under the fourteenth amendment to the Constitution. Led by Dr. Martin Luther King, Jr., the movement was at its strongest in the 1960s when it challenged the practice of racial segregation in the United States.

Desegregation: The process of ending the separation of people of different races in housing, schools, and public facilities.

Disruption of an adoption: The ending of an adoptive placement of a child before legal adoption occurs.

Foster care: The temporary placement of a child from a broken, abusive, or poor home in the care of a foster family.

Home study: The process of evaluating a prospective adoptive parent's ability to raise an adopted child.

Integration: A process in which diverse groups come together to create a harmonious multiracial society in which all enjoy equal rights.

North American Council on Adoptable Children (NACAC): A nonprofit coalition of adoptive parent support groups, citizen advocacy groups, caring individuals, and child-welfare agencies committed to meeting the needs of adoptable children in the United States and Canada.

Prejudice: A judgment formed beforehand; often an unfavorable, irrational opinion of members of a particular race, religion, or nationality.

Racism: An irrational belief in the superiority of a given group, people, or nation, usually one's own.

Transracial adoption: The adoption of a child of a race different from that of the adopting family.

FOR FURTHER READING

CHILDREN FOUR TO EIGHT YEARS OLD

Brodzinsky, Anne Braff. *The Mulberry Bird: Story of an Adoption*. Fort Wayne, Ind.: Perspective Press, 1986.

PRE-TEENS

Bunin, Catherine and Sherry. *Is That Your Sister? A True Story of Adoption*. New York: Pantheon Books, 1976.

Gabel, Susan. *Filling in the Blanks: A Guided Look at Growing Up Adopted*. Indianapolis: Perspectives Press, 1988.

Krementz, Jill. *How It Feels to Be Adopted*. New York: Knopf, 1985.

Lifton, Betty Jean. *I'm Still Me*. New York: Bantam Books, 1981.

Livingston, Carole. *Why Was I Adopted?* Secaucus, N.J.: Lyle Stuart, 1978.

Nerlove, Evelyn. *Who Is David? A Story of an Adopted Adolescent and His Friends*. Child Welfare League, 1985.

Powledge, Fred. *So You're Adopted*. New York: Scribner's, 1982.

Rosenberg, Maxine B. *Being Adopted*. New York: Lothrop, Lee and Shepard, 1984.

ADOPTIVE PARENTS

Dorris, Michael. *The Broken Cord*. New York: Harper & Row, 1989.

Fiegelman, W., and A. R. Silverman. *Chosen Children: New Patterns of Adoptive Relationships*. New York: Praeger, 1983.

Jewett, Claudia L. *Adopting the Older Child*. Cambridge: Harvard Common Press, 1978.

_____. *Helping Children Cope with Separation and Loss*. Cambridge: Harvard Common Press, 1982.

McNamara, Joan, and Bernard H. McNamara, editors. *Adoption and the Sexually Abused Child*. Bangor: University of Southern Maine Press, 1990.

Magid, Ken, and Carole A. McKelvey. *High Risk: Children Without a Conscience*. New York: Bantam Books, 1987.

Melina, Lois Ruskai. *Raising Adopted Children: A Manual for Adoptive Parents*. New York: Harper & Row, 1986.

_____. *Making Sense of Adoption*. New York: Harper & Row, 1989.

Schaffer, Judith, and Christine Lindstrom. *How to Raise an Adopted Child*. New York: Crown, 1989.

PARENTS OF AFRICAN AMERICAN CHILDREN

Adoff, Arnold. *Black Is Brown Is Tan*. New York: Harper & Row, 1973.

Comer, M. D., James P. Poussaint, and Alvin F. Poussaint. *Black Child Care: How to Bring Up a Healthy*

Black Child in America. New York: Simon & Schuster, 1975.

Harrison-Ross, M. D., Phyllis Wyden, and Barbara Wyden. *The Black Child: A Parents' Guide*. New York: Peter H. Wyden, 1973.

Hopson, Derek S., and Darlene Powell-Hopson. *Different and Wonderful: Raising Black Children in a Race-conscious Society*. Englewood Cliffs, NJ: Prentice Hall, 1990.

INDEX

ABOUT THE AUTHORS

Constance Pohl, a white parent of a nonwhite adopted son and a white biological daughter, is also a former foster parent. For many years she was a teacher in college and high school, before becoming a freelance editor of young adult books.

Kathy Harris, MSW, a white adoptive parent of four African American children, has professional as well as personal experience in transracial adoption. Since receiving her master's degree in social work, she has been a counselor with an agency for international adoptions, a foster care caseworker, and a pediatric social worker. She is now Supervisor of Adoption Services at Children's Aid and Adoption Society in New Jersey.

69407